The Mason Jar Cookbook

Discover the Convenience and Versatility of Mason Jar Meals with Over 100 Delicious Recipes

Ashley Clark

Copyright Material ©2023

All Rights Reserved

Without the proper written consent of the publisher and copyright owner, this book cannot be used or distributed in any way, shape, or form, except for brief quotations used in a review. This book should not be considered a substitute for medical, legal, or other professional advice.

TABLE OF CONTENTS

- **TABLE OF CONTENTS** 3
- **INTRODUCTION** 8
- **MASON JAR BREAKFAST** 9
  - 1. Mason jar chia puddings 10
  - 2. Rainbow Lime Chia Pudding 12
  - 3. Tropical Coconut Chia Pudding 14
  - 4. Berry Breakfast Parfait 16
- **MASON JAR MAINS** 18
  - 5. Mason jar chicken and ramen soup 19
  - 6. Mason jar bolognese 21
  - 7. Mason jar lasagna 23
  - 8. Mason jar beet and brussels sprout grain bowls 26
  - 9. Mason jar broccoli salad 28
  - 10. Mason jar chicken salad 30
  - 11. Mason jar Chinese chicken salad 32
  - 12. Mason jar niçoise salad 34
  - 13. Very green mason jar salad 36
- **MASON JAR SAUCES AND BROTH** 38
  - 14. Chimichurri Sauce 39
  - 15. Beef Bone Broth 41
  - 16. Kiwi daiquiri jam 43
  - 17. Crock Pot Dulce de Leche 45
  - 18. Louisiana-style hot sauce 47
  - 19. Chimichurri verde 49
  - 20. Ají amarillo sauce 51

21. Garlicky green chili sauce 53

22. Chipotle hot sauce 55

23. Ají picante 57

24. Apple Vinegar 59

25. Pineapple Vinegar 62

MASON JAR VEGGIES **64**

26. Dill pickles 65

27. Sauerkraut 67

28. Bread-and-butter pickles 69

29. Dill pickles 71

30. Sweet gherkin pickles 73

31. 14-Day sweet pickles 75

32. Quick sweet pickles 77

33. Pickled asparagus 79

34. Pickled dilled beans 81

35. Pickled three-bean salad 83

36. Pickled beets 85

37. Pickled carrots 87

38. Pickled cauliflower/Brussels 89

39. Chayote and jicama slaw 91

40. Bread-and-butter pickled jicama 93

41. Marinated whole mushrooms 95

42. Pickled dilled okra 97

43. Pickled pearl onions 99

44. Marinated peppers 101

45. Pickled bell peppers 103

46. Pickled hot peppers 105

47. Pickled jalapeño pepper rings 107
48. Pickled yellow pepper rings 109
49. Pickled sweet green tomatoes 111
50. Pickled mixed vegetables 113
51. Pickled bread-and-butter zucchini 115
52. Chayote and pear relish 117
53. Piccalilli 119
54. Pickle relish 121
55. Pickled corn relish 123
56. Pickled green tomato relish 125
57. Pickled horseradish sauce 127
58. Pickled pepper-onion relish 129
59. Spicy jicama relish 131
60. Tangy tomatillo relish 133
61. No sugar added pickled beets 135
62. Sweet pickle cucumber 137
63. Sliced dill pickles 139
64. Sliced sweet pickles 141
65. Lemon & Dill Kraut 143
66. Chinese Kimchi 145
67. Fermented Carrot Sticks 147
68. Carrots with an Indian Twist 149
69. Radish Bombs 151

MASON JAR DESSERT 153

70. Cadbury Egg Trifles 154
71. Raw Parfait with Spirulina Milk 156
72. Blueberry lemon cheesecake oats 158

73. Lime Flax Pudding 160

74. Individual Key Lime Cheesecakes 162

75. Coconut Raspberry Curd 165

76. Crème with Almond and Chocolate 167

77. Classic Holiday Custard 169

78. Chocolate Cream 171

79. Tzatziki 173

80. Creamy French Onion Dip 175

81. Green Salad with Peaches & Chèvre 177

82. Coconut Cream Cheese 179

83. Pear Crêpes with Macadamia Cheese 181

84. Gingerbread Cookie Ice Cream Sandwiches 184

85. Cultured Vanilla Ice Cream 186

86. Pumpkin Pie Ice Cream 188

87. Black Cherry Ice Cream 190

88. Orange Creamsicle Cheesecake 192

89. Pomegranate Cheesecake 194

90. Blackberry Cheesecake 196

91. Sweet Vanilla Peaches 198

MASON JAR DRINKS 200

92. Lemon and Cucumber Cooler 201

93. Vegan Kefir 203

94. Black Tea Kombucha 205

95. African Red Tea Kombucha 208

96. Cultured Bloody Mary 211

97. Peach Iced Tea 213

98. Watermelon Agua Fresca 215

99. Blueberry Lemonade 217
100. Mango Lassi 219
CONCLUSION 221

INTRODUCTION

Welcome to the wonderful world of mason jars! These versatile jars are not just for storing food or preserving fruits and vegetables. In fact, they can be used to create a wide range of delicious recipes that are both convenient and healthy. Whether you're looking to meal prep, pack a lunch, or make a dessert, mason jars are the perfect solution.

This cookbook features over 100 creative and easy-to-follow recipes that can all be made in mason jars. From breakfast to dinner, and even snacks and desserts, there's a recipe for every occasion. Plus, using mason jars means less waste and easier cleanup!

Discover the joys of layering ingredients to create visually stunning salads and grain bowls, or whip up a batch of overnight oats for an effortless breakfast. And let's not forget about the endless possibilities for desserts, like individual servings of cheesecake or brownies.

With this cookbook, you'll learn the ins and outs of using mason jars for cooking and meal prep. Whether you're a seasoned pro or new to the world of mason jars, you'll find plenty of inspiration and ideas for delicious and healthy meals..

MASON JAR BREAKFAST

1. **Mason jar chia puddings**

Ingredients
- 1 ¼ cups 2% milk
- 1 cup 2% plain Greek yogurt
- ½ cup chia seeds
- 2 tablespoons honey
- 2 tablespoons sugar
- 1 tablespoon orange zest
- 2 teaspoons vanilla extract
- ¾ cup segmented oranges
- ¾ cup segmented tangerines
- ½ cup segmented grapefruit

Directions

a) In a large bowl, whisk together the milk, Greek yogurt, chia seeds, honey, sugar, orange zest, vanilla, and salt until well combined.

b) Divide mixture evenly into four (16-ounce) mason jars. Refrigerate overnight, or up to 5 days.

c) Serve cold, topped with oranges, tangerines, and grapefruit.

2. Rainbow Lime Chia Pudding

Ingredients

- 1 ¼ cups 2% milk
- 1 cup 2% plain Greek yogurt
- ½ cup chia seeds
- 2 tablespoons honey
- 2 tablespoons sugar
- 2 teaspoons lime zest
- 2 tablespoons freshly squeezed lime juice
- 1 teaspoon vanilla extract
- 1 cup chopped strawberries and blueberries
- ½ cup diced mango and ½ cup diced kiwi

Directions

a) In a large bowl, whisk together the milk, yogurt, chia seeds, honey, sugar, lime zest, lime juice, vanilla, and salt until well combined.
b) Divide the mixture evenly into four (16-ounce) mason jars. Cover and refrigerate overnight, or up to 5 days.
c) Serve cold, topped with strawberries, mango, kiwi, and blueberries.

3. Tropical Coconut Chia Pudding

Ingredients
- 1 (13.5-ounce) can coconut milk
- 1 cup 2% plain Greek yogurt
- ½ cup chia seeds
- 2 tablespoons honey
- 2 tablespoons sugar
- 1 teaspoon vanilla extract
- Pinch of kosher salt
- 1 cup diced mango
- 1 cup diced pineapple
- 2 tablespoons shredded coconut

Directions

a) In a large bowl, whisk together the coconut milk, yogurt, chia seeds, honey, sugar, vanilla, and salt until well combined.

b) Divide the mixture evenly into four (16-ounce) mason jars. Cover and refrigerate overnight, or up to 5 days.

c) Serve cold, topped with mango and pineapple and sprinkled with coconut.

4. Berry Breakfast Parfait

Makes: 4

INGREDIENTS:
- 1½ cups low-fat plain yogurt
- 3 tablespoons honey
- 1½ cups muesli breakfast cereal or low-sodium, low-fat granola
- 1½ cups mixed fresh berries

INSTRUCTIONS:
a) Set out 4 parfait glasses, 8-ounce mason jars, or other 8-ounce glasses.
b) In a small mixing bowl, combine the yogurt and honey and stir to mix well.
c) Spoon 2 tablespoons of the yogurt mixture into the bottom of each glass or jar. Top with 2 tablespoons of the cereal, and then 2 tablespoons of the fruit. Repeat until all of the ingredients have been used.
d) Serve immediately or cover and refrigerate the parfaits for up to 2 hours.

MASON JAR MAINS

5. Mason jar chicken and ramen soup

Ingredients

- 2 (5.6-ounce) packages refrigerated yakisoba noodles
- 2 ½ tablespoons reduced-sodium vegetable broth base concentrate (we like Better Than Bouillon)
- 1 ½ tablespoons reduced-sodium soy sauce
- 1 tablespoon rice wine vinegar
- 1 tablespoon freshly grated ginger
- 2 teaspoons sambal oelek (ground fresh chile paste), or more to taste
- 2 teaspoons sesame oil
- 2 cups leftover shredded rotisserie chicken
- 3 cups baby spinach
- 2 carrots, peeled and grated
- 1 cup sliced shiitake mushrooms
- ½ cup fresh cilantro leaves
- 2 green onions, thinly sliced
- 1 teaspoon sesame seeds

Directions

a) In a large pot of boiling water, cook the yakisoba until loosened, 1 to 2 minutes; drain well.
b) In a small bowl, combine the broth base, soy sauce, vinegar, ginger, sambal oelek, and sesame oil.
c) Divide the broth mixture into 4 (24-ounce) wide-mouth glass jars with lids, or other heatproof containers. Top with yakisoba, chicken, spinach, carrots, mushrooms, cilantro, green onions, and sesame seeds. Cover and refrigerate for up to 4 days.
d) To serve, uncover a jar and add enough hot water to cover the contents, about 1 ¼ cups. Microwave, uncovered, until heated through, 2 to 3 minutes. Let stand 5 minutes, stir to combine, and serve immediately.

6. <u>**Mason jar bolognese**</u>

Ingredients

- 2 tablespoons olive oil
- 1-pound ground beef
- 1 pound Italian sausage, casings removed
- 1 onion, minced
- 4 cloves garlic, minced
- 3 (14.5-ounce) cans diced tomatoes, drained
- 2 (15-ounce) cans tomato sauce
- 3 bay leaves
- 1 teaspoon dried oregano
- 1 teaspoon dried basil
- ½ teaspoon dried thyme
- 1 teaspoon kosher salt
- ½ teaspoon freshly ground black pepper
- 2 (16-ounce) packages reduced-fat mozzarella cheese, cubed
- 32 ounces uncooked whole wheat fusilli, cooked according to package instructions; about 16 cups cooked

Directions

a) Heat the olive oil in a large skillet over medium-high heat. Add the ground beef, sausage, onion, and garlic. Cook until browned, 5 to 7 minutes, making sure to crumble the beef and sausage as it cooks; drain excess fat.

b) Transfer the ground beef mixture to a 6-quart slow cooker. Stir in the tomatoes, tomato sauce, bay leaves, oregano, basil, thyme, salt, and pepper. Cover and cook on low heat for 7 hours and 45 minutes. Remove the lid and turn the slow cooker to high. Continue to cook for 15 minutes, until the sauce has thickened. Discard the bay leaves and let the sauce cool completely.

c) Divide sauce into 16 (24-ounce) wide-mouth glass jars with lids, or other heatproof containers. Top with mozzarella and fusilli. Refrigerate for up to 4 days.

d) To serve, microwave, uncovered, until heated through, about 2 minutes. Stir to combine.

7. **Mason jar lasagna**

Ingredients
- 3 lasagna noodles
- 1 tablespoon olive oil
- ½ pound ground sirloin
- 1 onion, diced
- 2 cloves garlic, minced
- 3 tablespoons tomato paste
- 1 teaspoon Italian seasoning
- 2 (14.5-ounce) cans diced tomatoes
- 1 medium zucchini, grated
- 1 large carrot, grated
- 2 cups shredded baby spinach
- Kosher salt and freshly ground black pepper, to taste
- 1 cup part-skim ricotta cheese
- 1 cup shredded mozzarella cheese, divided
- 2 tablespoons chopped fresh basil leaves

Directions

a) In a large pot of boiling salted water, cook the pasta according to package instructions; drain well. Cut each noodle into 4 pieces; set aside.

b) Heat the olive oil in a large skillet or Dutch oven over medium-high heat. Add the ground sirloin and onion and cook until browned, 3 to 5 minutes, making sure to crumble the beef as it cooks; drain excess fat.

c) Stir in the garlic, tomato paste, and Italian seasoning and cook until fragrant, 1 to 2 minutes. Stir in the tomatoes, reduce the heat, and simmer until slightly thickened, 5 to 6 minutes. Stir in the zucchini, carrot, and spinach and cook, stirring frequently, until tender, 2 to 3 minutes. Season with salt and pepper to taste. Set sauce aside.

d) In a small bowl, combine the ricotta, ½ cup of the mozzarella, and the basil; season with salt and pepper to taste

e) Preheat the oven to 375 degrees F. Lightly oil 4 (16-ounce) wide-mouth glass jars with lids, or other oven-safe containers, or coat with nonstick spray.

f) Place 1 pasta piece into each jar. Divide one-third of the sauce into the jars. Repeat with a second layer of pasta and sauce. Top with ricotta mixture, remaining pasta, and remaining sauce. Sprinkle with remaining ½ cup mozzarella cheese.
g) Set the jars on a baking sheet. Place in the oven and bake until bubbling, 25 to 30 minutes; cool completely. Refrigerate for up to 4 days.

8. Mason jar beet and brussels sprout grain bowls

Ingredients
- 3 medium beets (about 1 pound)
- 1 tablespoon olive oil
- Kosher salt and freshly ground black pepper, to taste
- 1 cup farro
- 4 cups baby spinach or kale
- 2 cups Brussels sprouts (about 8 ounces), thinly sliced
- 3 clementines, peeled and segmented
- ½ cup pecans, toasted
- ½ cup pomegranate seeds

Honey-Dijon red wine vinaigrette
- ¼ cup extra-virgin olive oil
- 2 tablespoons red wine vinegar
- ½ shallot, minced
- 1 tablespoon honey
- 2 teaspoons whole grain mustard
- Kosher salt and freshly ground black pepper, to taste

Directions
a) Preheat the oven to 400 degrees F. Line a baking sheet with foil.
b) Place the beets on the foil, drizzle with olive oil, and season with salt and pepper. Fold up all 4 sides of the foil to make a pouch. Bake until fork-tender, 35 to 45 minutes; let cool, about 30 minutes.
c) Using a clean paper towel, rub the beets to remove the skins; dice into bite-size pieces.
d) Cook the farro according to package Directions, then let cool.
e) Divide the beets into 4 (32-ounce) wide-mouth glass jars with lids. Top with spinach or kale, farro, Brussels sprouts, clementines, pecans, and pomegranate seeds. Will keep covered in the refrigerator 3 or 4 days.
f) FOR THE VINAIGRETTE: Whisk together the olive oil, vinegar, shallot, honey, mustard, and 1 tablespoon water; season with salt and pepper to taste. Cover and refrigerate for up to 3 days.
g) To serve, add the vinaigrette to each jar and shake. Serve immediately.

9. Mason jar broccoli salad

Ingredients
- 3 tablespoons 2% milk
- 2 tablespoons olive oil mayonnaise
- 2 tablespoons Greek yogurt
- 1 tablespoon sugar, or more to taste
- 2 teaspoons apple cider vinegar
- ½ cup cashews
- ¼ cup dried cranberries
- ½ cup diced red onion
- 2 ounces' cheddar cheese, diced
- 5 cups coarsely chopped broccoli florets

Directions

a) FOR THE DRESSING: Whisk together the milk, mayonnaise, yogurt, sugar, and vinegar in a small bowl.

b) Divide the dressing into 4 (16-ounce) wide-mouth glass jars with lids. Top with cashews, cranberries, onion, cheese, and broccoli. Refrigerate for up to 3 days.

c) To serve, shake the contents of a jar and serve immediately.

10. Mason jar chicken salad

Ingredients
- 2 ½ cups leftover shredded rotisserie chicken
- ½ cup Greek yogurt
- 2 tablespoons olive oil mayonnaise
- ¼ cup diced red onion
- 1 stalk celery, diced
- 1 tablespoon freshly squeezed lemon juice, or more to taste
- 1 teaspoon chopped fresh tarragon
- ½ teaspoon Dijon mustard
- ½ teaspoon garlic powder
- Kosher salt and freshly ground black pepper, to taste
- 4 cups shredded kale
- 2 Granny Smith apples, cored and chopped
- ½ cup cashews
- ½ cup dried cranberries

Directions

a) In a large bowl, combine the chicken, yogurt, mayonnaise, red onion, celery, lemon juice, tarragon, mustard, and garlic powder; season with salt and pepper to taste.

b) Divide the chicken mixture into 4 (24-ounce) wide-mouth glass jars with lids. Top with kale, apples, cashews, and cranberries. Refrigerate for up to 3 days.

c) To serve, shake contents of a jar and serve immediately.

11. Mason jar Chinese chicken salad

Ingredients
- ½ cup rice wine vinegar
- 2 cloves garlic, pressed
- 1 tablespoon sesame oil
- 1 tablespoon freshly grated ginger
- 2 teaspoons sugar, or more to taste
- ½ teaspoon reduced-sodium soy sauce
- 2 green onions, thinly sliced
- 1 teaspoon sesame seeds
- 2 carrots, peeled and grated
- 2 cups diced English cucumber
- 2 cups shredded purple cabbage
- 12 cups chopped kale
- 1 ½ cups leftover diced rotisserie chicken
- 1 cup wonton strips

Directions

a) FOR THE VINAIGRETTE: Whisk together the vinegar, garlic, sesame oil, ginger, sugar, and soy sauce in a small bowl. Divide the dressing into 4 (32-ounce) wide-mouth glass jars with lids.

b) Top with green onions, sesame seeds, carrots, cucumber, cabbage, kale, and chicken. Refrigerate for up to 3 days. Store the wonton strips separately.

c) To serve, shake contents of a jar and add the wonton strips. Serve immediately.

12. Mason jar niçoise salad

Ingredients
- 2 medium eggs
- 2 ½ cups halved green beans
- 3 (7-ounce) cans albacore tuna packed in water, drained and rinsed
- ¼ cup extra-virgin olive oil
- 2 tablespoons red wine vinegar
- 2 tablespoons diced red onion
- 2 tablespoons chopped fresh parsley leaves
- 1 tablespoon chopped fresh tarragon leaves
- 1 ½ teaspoons Dijon mustard
- Kosher salt and freshly ground black pepper, to taste
- 1 cup halved cherry tomatoes
- 4 cups torn butter lettuce
- 3 cups arugula leaves
- 12 Kalamata olives
- 1 lemon, cut into wedges (optional)

Directions

a) Place the eggs in a large saucepan and cover with cold water by 1 inch. Bring to a boil and cook for 1 minute. Cover the pot with a tight-fitting lid and remove from the heat; let sit for 8 to 10 minutes.

b) Meanwhile, in a large pot of boiling salted water, blanch the green beans until bright green in color, about 2 minutes. Drain and cool in a bowl of ice water. Drain well. Drain the eggs and let cool before peeling and cutting the eggs in half lengthwise.

c) In a large bowl, combine the tuna, olive oil, vinegar, onion, parsley, tarragon, and Dijon until just combined; season with salt and pepper to taste.

d) Divide the tuna mixture into 4 (32-ounce) wide-mouth glass jars with lids. Top with green beans, eggs, tomatoes, butter lettuce, arugula, and olives. Refrigerate for up to 3 days.

e) To serve, shake contents of a jar. Serve immediately, with lemon wedges if desired.

13. Very green mason jar salad

Ingredients

- ¾ cup pearled barley
- 1 cup fresh basil leaves
- ¾ cup 2% Greek yogurt
- 2 green onions, chopped
- 1 ½ tablespoons freshly squeezed lime juice
- 1 clove garlic, peeled
- Kosher salt and freshly ground black pepper, to taste
- ½ English cucumber, coarsely chopped
- 1 pound (4 small) zucchini, spiralized
- 4 cups shredded kale
- 1 cup frozen green peas, thawed
- ½ cup crumbled reduced-fat feta cheese
- ½ cup pea shoots
- 1 lime, cut into wedges (optional)

Directions

a) Cook the barley according to package instructions; let cool completely and set aside.
b) To make the dressing, combine the basil, yogurt, green onions, lime juice, and garlic in the bowl of a food processor and season with salt and pepper. Pulse until smooth, about 30 seconds to 1 minute.
c) Divide the dressing into 4 (32-ounce) wide mouth glass jars with lids. Top with cucumber, zucchini noodles, barley, kale, peas, feta, and pea shoots. Refrigerate for up to 3 days.
d) To serve, shake the contents in a jar. Serve immediately, with lime wedges, if desired.

MASON JAR SAUCES AND BROTH

14. Chimichurri Sauce

INGREDIENTS:
- 1 cup lightly packed fresh parsley
- ¼ cup organic red wine vinegar
- 2 large cloves garlic
- ¼ cup extra-virgin olive oil
- 1 teaspoon dried thyme
- ½ teaspoon salt
- ¼ teaspoon red pepper flakes
- ⅛ teaspoon freshly ground black pepper
- ¼ cup Beef Bone Broth
- ¼ ripe avocado

INSTRUCTIONS:
a) Place all ingredients in a food processor, blend for about 30 seconds or until all ingredients are combined well. If it's too thin to your liking, add more avocado. If it's too thick, add more beef bone broth.
b) Pour the chimichurri sauce into an 8-ounce mason jar. Cover and store in the fridge for up to 2 weeks.

15. Beef Bone Broth

INGREDIENTS:
- 3-4 pounds of mixed grass-fed beef bones
- 2 medium onions, chopped
- 2 medium carrots, chopped
- 3 celery stalks, chopped
- 2 bay leaves
- 2 tablespoons apple cider vinegar
- 1 tablespoon peppercorns
- 8-10 cups water

INSTRUCTIONS:

a) Heat oven to 400°F.

b) Place the mixed bones in a roasting pan in a single layer and place it into the oven. Roast the bones for 30 minutes. Turn bones over and roast another 30 minutes.

c) While the bones are roasting, chop the carrots, onions and celery. You are going to discard these after long hours of cooking, so a rough chop works great!

d) Place roasted bones, chopped vegetables, bay leaves, apple cider vinegar and peppercorns in a 6-quart crockpot. Cover completely with water.

e) Cover and cook on low for 24 hours. Add water as needed to keep all the ingredients covered in water and periodically skim the foam off the top of the pot.

f) After 24 hours, the broth should be a dark brown color. Discard all solids and strain the broth through a fine mesh strainer into a large bowl. Strain once more through cheesecloth to remove any remaining particles if desired.

g) Ladle the bone broth into Mason jars and let it chill to room temperature. Bone broth can be stored in the fridge for up to two weeks or frozen for future use. Before using, skim off the accumulated fat on the surface.

16. Kiwi daiquiri jam

Makes: 4 servings

INGREDIENTS:
- 5 Kiwifruit, peeled
- 3 cups Sugar
- ⅔ cup Unsweetened pineapple juice
- ⅓ cup Fresh lime juice
- 3 ounces liquid pectin
- Green food color, optional
- 4 tablespoons Rum

INSTRUCTIONS:
a) Fill the boiling water canner with water. Place 4 clean half-pint mason jars in the canner. Cover, bring water to a boil, and boil for at least 10 min to sterilize jars at altitudes up to 1000 ft.
b) Place snap lids in boiling water, and boil for 5 min to soften the sealing compound.
c) In a large stainless steel or enamel saucepan, mash kiwifruit to an applesauce consistency. Stir in sugar, pineapple, and lime juice.
d) Bring to a full rolling boil, stirring until sugar dissolves.
e) Stirring constantly, boil vigorously for 2 minutes.
f) Remove from heat, and stir in pectin. Continue stirring for 5 minutes to prevent floating fruit. Stir in rum.
g) Ladle jam into a hot sterilized jar to within ¼ inch of the top rim.
h) Remove air bubbles by sliding a rubber spatula between glass and food, and readjust the head space to ¼ inch. Wipe the jar rim removing any stickiness. Center snap lid on the jar, apply screw band just until fingertip tight. Place jar in canner. Repeat for the remaining jam.
i) Cover the canner, return the water to a boil, and process for 5 minutes. Cool 24 hours. Check jar seals.
j) Remove screw bands. Wipe jars, label and store them in a cool dark place.

17. Crock Pot Dulce de Leche

Makes: 16

INGREDIENTS:
- 2 (14-ounce) cans of sweetened condensed milk

INSTRUCTIONS:
a) Fill the Mason jars to the brim with sweetened condensed milk.
b) Screw the lids on tightly.
c) Place upright in a slow cooker.
d) Fill the crock pot halfway with hot tap water to cover the jars.
e) Cook on LOW for 8 to 10 hours.
f) Allow cooling to room temperature on the counter.
g) Refrigerate until needed.

18. Louisiana-style hot sauce

MAKES 16 OUNCES

Ingredients:
- 1 pound (about 10) fresh cayenne or tabasco peppers, stemmed
- 2 teaspoons non-iodized salt
- ½ cup white wine vinegar or white vinegar
- 2 garlic cloves

Directions:

a) In a blender or food processor, combine the chiles and salt. Blend until a mash forms and a brine releases from the chiles.

b) Pack the mash into a clean jar and press it down until the natural brine covers the chiles, leaving at least 1 inch of headspace.

c) Place a cartouche, if using, then screw the lid on tightly and store the jar at room temperature away from direct sunlight to ferment for 2 weeks. Burp the jar daily.

d) Once fermentation is complete, combine the mash (natural brine included), vinegar, and garlic in a food processor or blender. Blend until the sauce is as smooth as possible.

e) Store the hot sauce in an airtight container in the refrigerator for up to 1 year.

19. Chimichurri verde

MAKES 8 OUNCES

Ingredients:
- 2 cups freshly chopped parsley
- 1 cup freshly chopped cilantro
- 2 scallions, both white and green parts, chopped
- 4 garlic cloves, minced
- 1 fresh red chile (such as cayenne or tabasco), stemmed and chopped
- 1½ teaspoons non-iodized salt
- ¼ cup red wine vinegar
- ¼ cup olive oil, for serving

Directions:
a) In a mixing bowl, combine the parsley, cilantro, scallions, garlic, and red chile. Sprinkle with the salt. Using your hands, massage the salt into the veggies. Let it sit for 10 minutes to allow a brine to form.
a) Once the natural brine has been released, pack the mixture and brine into a clean jar. Press the mixture down until the brine covers the veggies.
b) Place a cartouche, if using, then screw the lid on tightly and store the jar at room temperature away from direct sunlight to ferment for 5 days. Burp the jar daily.
c) Once fermentation is complete, combine the ferment and red wine vinegar in a blender or food processor. Blend until well combined.
d) Store the chimichurri in the refrigerator for up to 3 months. When ready to serve, add 1 tablespoon of olive oil per ¼ cup of chimichurri.

20. Ají amarillo sauce

MAKES 16 OUNCES

Ingredients:

For the paste
- 4 ounces (about 15) dried ají amarillo peppers, stemmed and torn into pieces
- 6 garlic cloves
- 3 scallions, both white and green parts, sliced
- 2½ cups non-chlorinated water
- 2 tablespoons non-iodized salt
- 5 tablespoons lime juice
- 2 tablespoons reserved brine

For the sauce
- 2 cups ají amarillo paste
- 1 cup evaporated milk
- 1 cup queso fresco or feta cheese
- ¼ cup crushed crackers or bread crumbs

Directions:

a) To make the paste: In a clean jar, combine the chiles, garlic, and scallions.
b) In a separate vessel, make a brine by combining the water and salt.
c) Place a weight, if using, then pour the brine into the jar, leaving at least 1 inch of headspace. Screw the lid on tightly and store the jar at room temperature away from direct sunlight to ferment for 10 days. Burp the jar daily.
d) Once fermentation is complete, strain the ferment, reserving 2 tablespoons of the brine.
e) In a blender or food processor, combine the ferment, lime juice, and reserved brine. Blend until smooth.
f) Store the paste in the fridge for up to 6 months.
g) To make the sauce: In a blender or food processor, combine the ají amarillo paste, evaporated milk, cheese, and crackers or bread crumbs.
h) Blend until smooth.

21. Garlicky green chili sauce

MAKES 16 OUNCES

Ingredients:
- 1 pound (about 6) fresh Hatch chiles, stemmed
- 8 garlic cloves
- 2 teaspoons non-iodized salt
- 2 teaspoons cumin seeds
- 1 teaspoon ground oregano
- ¼ cup white vinegar
- 1 tablespoon granulated sugar

Directions:
a) In a blender or food processor, combine the chiles, garlic, salt, cumin seeds, and oregano. Blend until roughly chopped and a natural brine has been released. Pour the mixture into a clean jar.
b) Place a cartouche, if using, then screw the lid on tightly and store the jar at room temperature away from direct sunlight to ferment for 5 days. Burp the jar daily.
c) Once fermentation is complete, combine the ferment, vinegar, and sugar in a food processor or blender. Blend until smooth.
d) Store the sauce in the refrigerator for up to 1 year.

22. Chipotle hot sauce

MAKES 16 OUNCES

Ingredients:
- 2 ounces (about 15) dried chipotle peppers, stemmed
- 6 garlic cloves
- ½ white or yellow onion, halved
- 2 cups non-chlorinated water
- 1 tablespoon plus 1 teaspoon non-iodized salt
- ½ cup orange juice
- ½ cup apple cider vinegar
- ¼ cup reserved brine
- 2 tablespoons tomato paste
- 1 tablespoon granulated sugar
- 1 teaspoon cumin seeds

Directions:
a) In a clean jar, combine the chiles, garlic, and onion.
b) In a separate vessel, make a brine by combining the water and salt.
c) Place a weight, if using, then pour the brine into the jar, leaving at least 1 inch of headspace. Screw the lid on tightly and store the jar at room temperature away from direct sunlight to ferment for 1 week. Burp the jar daily.
d) Once fermentation is complete, strain the ferment, reserving ¼ cup of the brine.
e) In a blender or food processor, combine the ferment, orange juice, vinegar, reserved brine, tomato paste, sugar, and cumin seeds. Blend until smooth.
f) Keep the sauce stored in the refrigerator for up to 1 year.

23. Ají picante

MAKES 16 OUNCES

Ingredients:
- 1 ounce (about 4) fresh ají chirca or habanero peppers, stemmed and chopped
- 6 scallions, both white and green parts, chopped
- 1 cup freshly chopped cilantro
- 2 medium tomatoes, chopped
- 1 tablespoon non-iodized salt
- 1 cup water
- ¼ cup reserved brine
- ¼ cup white vinegar
- 2 tablespoons lime juice
- 2 teaspoons granulated sugar
- ¼ cup avocado or sunflower oil, for serving

Directions:
a) In a mixing bowl, combine the chiles, scallions, cilantro, and tomatoes. Sprinkle the vegetables with the salt.
b) Using your hands, massage the salt into the veggies until a brine begins to form. Let the veggies sit for 30 minutes, or until enough brine has formed to cover the ingredients in a jar.
c) Pack the mash into a clean jar, pressing it down to ensure the brine covers the mash.
d) Place a cartouche, if using, then screw the lid on tightly and store the jar at room temperature to ferment for 5 days. Burp the jar daily.
e) Once fermentation is complete, strain the mash, reserving ¼ cup of the brine.
f) Combine the mash, water, reserved brine, vinegar, lime juice, and sugar in a food processor or blender. Pulse lightly until combined well but not pureed completely. For a slightly chunkier version, you can skip the pulsing step and simply mix the ingredients by hand.
g) Keep the ají picante stored in an airtight container in the refrigerator for up to 1 year.
h) Mix in 1 tablespoon of oil per 1 cup of sauce right before serving.

24. Apple Vinegar

Makes about ½ to 1 quart/liter

Ingredients:
- ½ cup coconut sugar
- 1 quart filtered water
- 4 apples, cores and skins included

Directions:

a) In a pitcher or large measuring cup, mix together the sugar and water, stirring if necessary to encourage the sugar to dissolve.

b) Chop the apples into quarters, and then chop each piece in half. Place the apple pieces, cores and skins included, in a 1- to 2-quart jar or crock, leaving about 1 to 2 inches at the top of the jar.

c) Pour the sugar-water solution over the apples, leaving about ¾ inch at the top of the jar. The apples will float to the top, and some won't be submerged, but that's okay.

d) Cover the opening with a few layers of clean cheesecloth, and attach an elastic band around the mouth of the jar or crock to hold the cheesecloth in place.

e) Every day, remove the cheesecloth, and stir to cover the apples with the sugar-water solution, re-covering with the cheesecloth when you're done. You must do every day to ensure that the apples don't go moldy during the fermentation process.

f) After two weeks, strain off the apples, reserving the liquid; you can add the apples to your compost. Pour the liquid into a bottle, and seal with a tight-fitting lid or cork. The vinegar keeps for approximately one year.

g) Push them through an electric juicer to make apple juice. If you don't have a juicer, just cut the apples into quarters and puree them in a food processor

h) hen push the apple pulp through a muslin-lined sieve or muslin bag to remove the fiber from the juice.

i) Pour the juice into clean, dark, glass jugs or bottles without putting a lid on them. Cover the tops with a few layers of cheesecloth, and hold them in place with an elastic band.
j) Store the bottles or jars in a cool, dark place for three weeks to six months.

25. Pineapple Vinegar

Makes about ½ to 1 quart/liter

Ingredients:
a) ½ cup coconut sugar
b) 1 quart filtered water
c) 1 medium pineapple

Directions:
a) In a pitcher or large measuring cup, mix together the sugar and water, stirring if necessary to encourage the sugar to dissolve.
b) Remove the skin and core from the pineapple. Set the meat of the fruit aside for another use. Coarsely chop the skins and core. Place the pineapple scraps in a 1- to 2-quart jar or crock, leaving about 1 to 2 inches at the top of the jar.
c) Pour the sugar-water solution over the pineapple skins and core, leaving about ¾ inch at the top of the jar. The pieces will float to the top, and some won't be submerged, but that's okay.
d) Cover the opening with a few layers of clean cheesecloth, and attach an elastic band around the mouth of the jar or crock to hold the cheesecloth in place.
e) Every day, remove the cheesecloth, and stir to cover the pineapple pieces with the sugar-water solution. You must do every day to ensure that the pineapple pieces don't go moldy during the fermentation process.
f) After two weeks, strain off the pineapple pieces, reserving the liquid; you can add the pineapple to your compost. Pour the liquid into a bottle, and seal with a tight-fitting lid or cork. The vinegar keeps for approximately one year.

MASON JAR VEGGIES

26. Dill pickles

Ingredients:
- 4 lbs. of 4-inch pickling cucumber
- 2 Tablespoons dill seed or 4 to 5 heads fresh or dry dill wee
- 1/2 cup salt
- 1/4 cup vinegar (5%
- 8 cups water and one or more of the following ingredients:
- 2 cloves garlic (optional)
- 2 dried red peppers (optional)
- 2 teaspoons whole mixed pickling spices

Directions:

a) Wash cucumbers. Cut 1/16-inch slice of blossom end and discard. Leave 1/4-inch of stem attached. Place half of dill and spices on bottom of a clean, suitable container.

b) Add cucumbers, remaining dill, and spices. Dissolve salt in vinegar and water and pour over cucumbers.

c) Add suitable cover and weight. Store where temperature is between 70° and 75°F for about 3 to 4 weeks while fermenting. Temperatures of 55° to 65°F are acceptable, but the fermentation will take 5 to 6 weeks.

d) Avoid temperatures above 80°F, or pickles will become too soft during fermentation. Fermenting pickles cure slowly. Check the container several times a week and promptly remove surface scum or mold. Caution: If the pickles become soft, slimy, or develop a disagreeable odor, discard them.

e) Fully fermented pickles may be stored in the original container for about 4 to 6 months, provided they are refrigerated and surface scum and molds are removed regularly. Canning fully fermented pickles is a better way to store them. To can them, pour the brine into a pan, heat slowly to a boil, and simmer 5 minutes. Filter brine through paper coffee filters to reduce cloudiness, if desired.

f) Fill hot jar with pickles and hot brine, leaving 1/2-inch headspace.

g) Remove air bubbles and adjust headspace if needed. Wipe rims of jars with a dampened clean paper towel.

27. Sauerkraut

Ingredients:
- 25 lbs. cabbage
- 3/4 cup canning or pickling salt

Yield: About 9 quarts

Directions:

a) Work with about 5 pounds of cabbage at a time. Discard outer leaves. Rinse heads under cold running water and drain. Cut heads in quarters and remove cores. Shred or slice to a thickness of a quarter.

b) Put cabbage in a suitable fermentation container and add 3 tablespoons of salt. Mix thoroughly, using clean hands. Pack firmly until salt draws juices from cabbage.

c) Repeat shredding, salting, and packing until all cabbage is in the container. Be sure it is deep enough so that its rim is at least 4 or 5 inches above the cabbage. If juice does not cover cabbage, add boiled and cooled brine (1-1/2 tablespoons of salt per quart of water).

d) Add plate and weights; cover container with a clean bath towel.

e) If you weigh the cabbage down with a brine-filled bag, do not disturb the crock until normal fermentation is completed (when bubbling ceases). If you use jars as weight, you will have to check the kraut two to three times each week and remove scum if it forms. Fully fermented kraut may be kept tightly covered in the refrigerator for several months.

f) Remove air bubbles and adjust headspace if needed. Wipe rims of jars with a dampened clean paper towel.

28. Bread-and-butter pickles

Ingredients:
- 6 lbs. of 4- to 5-inch pickling cucumbers
- 8 cups thinly sliced onions
- 1/2 cup canning or pickling salt
- 4 cups vinegar (5%)
- 4-1/2 cups sugar
- 2 Tablespoons mustard seed
- 1-1/2 Tablespoons celery seed
- 1 Tablespoon ground turmeric
- 1 cup pickling lime

Yield: About 8 pints

Directions:

a) Wash cucumbers. Cut 1/16-inch of blossom end and discard. Cut into 3/16-inch slices. Combine cucumbers and onions in a large bowl. Add salt. Cover with 2 inches crushed or cubed ice. Refrigerate 3 to 4 hours, adding more ice as needed.

b) Combine remaining ingredients in a large pot. Boil 10 minutes. Drain and add cucumbers and onions and slowly reheat to boiling. Fill hot pint jars with slices and cooking syrup, leaving 1/2-inch headspace.

c) Remove air bubbles and adjust headspace if needed. Wipe rims of jars with a dampened clean paper towel.

29. Dill pickles

Ingredients:
- 8 lbs. of 3- to 5-inch pickling cucumbers
- 2 gallons water
- 1-1/4 cups canning or pickling salt
- 1-1/2 quarts vinegar (5%)
- 1/4 cup sugar
- 2 quarts water
- 2 Tablespoons whole mixed pickling spice
- about 3 Tablespoons whole mustard seed
- about 14 heads of fresh dill

Yield: About 7 to 9 pints

Directions:

a) Wash cucumbers. Cut 1/16-inch slice of blossom end and discard, but leave 1/4-inch of stem attached. Dissolve 3/4 cup salt in 2 gallons water. Pour over cucumbers and let stand 12 hours. Drain.

b) Combine vinegar, 1/2 cup salt, sugar, and 2 quarts water. Add mixed pickling spices tied in a clean white cloth. Heat to boiling. Fill hot jars with cucumbers.

c) Add 1 teaspoon mustard seed and 1-1/2 heads fresh dill per pint. Cover with boiling pickling solution, leaving 1/2-inch headspace. Remove air bubbles and adjust headspace if needed. Wipe rims of jars with a dampened clean paper towel.

30. Sweet gherkin pickles

Ingredients:
- 7 lbs. cucumbers (1-1/2 inch or less)
- 1/2 cup canning or pickling salt
- 8 cups sugar
- 6 cups vinegar (5%)
- 3/4 teaspoons turmeric
- 2 teaspoons celery seeds
- 2 teaspoons whole mixed pickling spice
- 2 cinnamon sticks
- 1/2 teaspoons fennel (optional)
- 2 teaspoons vanilla (optional)

Yield: About 6 to 7 pints

Directions:
a) Wash cucumbers. Cut 1/16-inch slice of blossom end and discard, but leave 1/4-inch of stem attached.
b) Place cucumbers in large container and cover with boiling water. Six to 8 hours later, and again on the second day, drain and cover with 6 quarts of fresh boiling water containing 1/4-cup salt. On the third day, drain and prick cucumbers with a table fork.
c) Combine and bring to a boil 3 cups vinegar, 3 cups sugar, turmeric, and spices. Pour over cucumbers. Six to 8 hours later, drain and save the pickling syrup. Add another 2 cups each of sugar and vinegar and reheat to boil. Pour over pickles.
d) On the fourth day, drain and save syrup. Add another 2 cups sugar and 1 cup vinegar. Heat to boiling and pour over pickles. Drain and save pickling syrup 6 to 8 hours later. Add 1 cup sugar and 2 teaspoons vanilla and heat to boiling.
e) Fill hot sterile pint jars with pickles and cover with hot syrup, leaving 1/2-inch headspace.
f) Remove air bubbles and adjust headspace if needed. Wipe rims of jars with a dampened clean paper towel.

31. 14-Day sweet pickles

Ingredients:
- 4 lbs. of 2- to 5-inch pickling cucumbers
- 3/4 cup canning or pickling salt
- 2 teaspoons celery seed
- 2 Tablespoons mixed pickling spices
- 5-1/2 cups sugar
- 4 cups vinegar (5%)

Yield: About 5 to 9 pints

Directions:
a) Wash cucumbers. Cut 1/16-inch slice of blossom end and discard, but leave 1/4-inch of stem attached. Place whole cucumbers in suitable 1-gallon container.
b) Add 1/4 cup canning or pickling salt to 2 quarts water and bring to a boil. Pour over cucumbers. Add suitable cover and weight.
c) Place clean towel over container and keep the temperature at about 70°F. On the third and fifth days, drain salt water and discard. Rinse cucumbers and return cucumbers to container. Add 1/4 cup salt to 2 quarts fresh water and boil. Pour over cucumbers.
d) Replace cover and weight, and re-cover with clean towel. On the seventh day, drain salt water and discard. Rinse cucumbers, cover, and weight.

32. Quick sweet pickles

Ingredients:
- 8 lbs. of 3- to 4-inch pickling cucumbers
- 1/3 cup canning or pickling salt
- 4-1/2 cups sugar
- 3-1/2 cups vinegar (5%)
- 2 teaspoons celery seed
- 1 Tablespoon whole allspice
- 2 Tablespoons mustard seed
- 1 cup pickling lime (optional)

Yield: About 7 to 9 pints

Directions:
a) Wash cucumbers. Cut 1/16-inch of blossom end and discard, but leave 1/4 inch of stem attached. Slice or cut in strips, if desired. Place in bowl and sprinkle with 1/3 cup salt. Cover with 2 inches of crushed or cubed ice.
b) Refrigerate 3 to 4 hours. Add more ice as needed. Drain well.
c) Combine sugar, vinegar, celery seed, allspice, and mustard seed in 6-quart kettle. Heat to boiling.
d) Hot pack—Add cucumbers and heat slowly until vinegar solution returns to boil. Stir occasionally to make sure mixture heats evenly. Fill sterile jars, leaving 1/2-inch headspace.
e) Raw pack—Fill hot jars, leaving 1/2-inch headspace. Add hot pickling syrup, leaving 1/2-inch headspace.
f) Remove air bubbles and adjust headspace if needed. Wipe rims of jars with a dampened clean paper towel.

33. **Pickled asparagus**

Ingredients:
- 10 lbs. asparagus
- 6 large garlic cloves
- 4-1/2 cups water
- 4-1/2 cups white distilled vinegar (5%)
- 6 small hot peppers (optional)
- 1/2 cup canning salt
- 3 teaspoons dill seed

Yield: 6 wide-mouth pint jars

Directions:
a) Wash asparagus well, but gently, under running water. Cut stems from the bottom to leave spears with tips that it into the canning jar, leaving a little more than 1/2-inch headspace. Peel and wash garlic cloves.
b) Place a garlic clove at the bottom of each jar, and tightly pack asparagus into hot jars with the blunt ends down. In an 8-quart saucepot, combine water, vinegar, hot peppers (optional), salt and dill seed.
c) Bring to a boil. Place one hot pepper (if used) in each jar over asparagus spears. Pour boiling hot pickling brine over spears, leaving 1/2-inch headspace.
d) Remove air bubbles and adjust headspace if needed. Wipe rims of jars with a dampened clean paper towel.

34. Pickled dilled beans

Ingredients:
- 4 lbs. fresh tender green or yellow beans
- 8 to 16 heads fresh dill
- 8 cloves garlic (optional)
- 1/2 cup canning or pickling salt
- 4 cups white vinegar (5%)
- 4 cups water
- 1 teaspoon hot red pepper flakes

Yield: About 8 pints

Directions:

a) Wash and trim ends from beans and cut to 4-inch lengths. In each hot sterile pint jar, place 1 to 2 dill heads and, if desired, 1 clove of garlic. Place whole beans upright in jars, leaving 1/2-inch headspace.

b) Trim beans to ensure proper it, if necessary. Combine salt, vinegar, water, and pepper flakes (if desired). Bring to a boil. Add hot solution to beans, leaving 1/2-inch headspace.

c) Remove air bubbles and adjust headspace if needed. Wipe rims of jars with a dampened clean paper towel.

35. Pickled three-bean salad

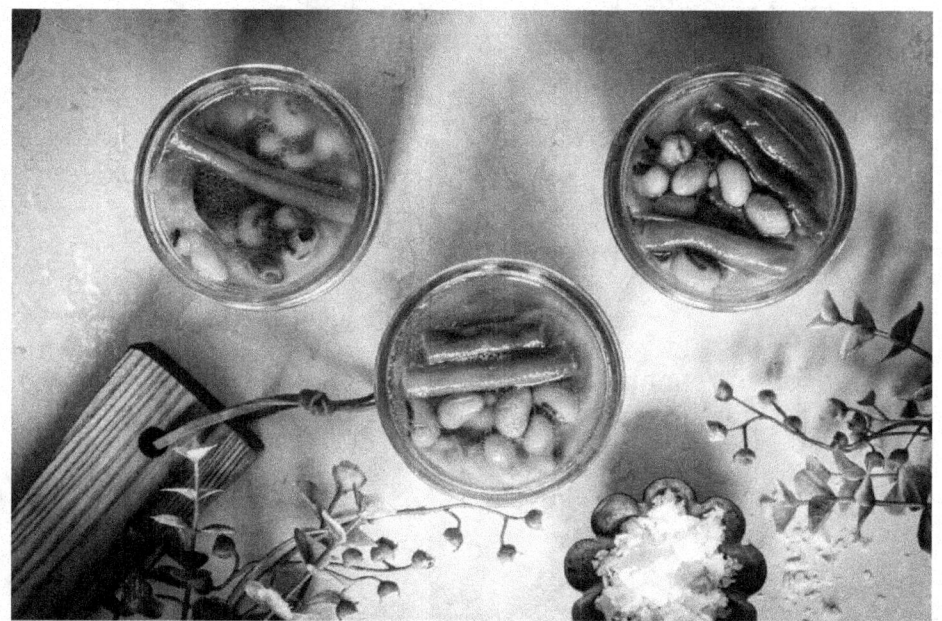

Ingredients:
- 1-1/2 cups blanched green/yellow beans
- 1-1/2 cups canned, drained, red kidney beans
- 1 cup canned, drained garbanzo beans
- 1/2 cup peeled and thinly sliced onion
- 1/2 cup trimmed and thinly sliced celery
- 1/2 cup sliced green peppers
- 1/2 cup white vinegar (5%)
- 1/4 cup bottled lemon juice
- 3/4 cup sugar
- 1/4 cup oil
- 1/2 teaspoons canning or pickling salt
- 1-1/4 cups water

Yield: About 5 to 6 half-pints

Directions:
a) Wash and snap of ends of fresh beans. Cut or snap into 1- to 2-inch pieces.
b) Blanch 3 minutes and cool immediately. Rinse kidney beans with tap water and drain again. Prepare and measure all other vegetables.
c) Combine vinegar, lemon juice, sugar, and water and bring to a boil. Remove from heat.
d) Add oil and salt and mix well. Add beans, onions, celery, and green pepper to solution and bring to a simmer.
e) Marinate 12 to 14 hours in refrigerator, then heat entire mixture to a boil. Fill hot jars with solids. Add hot liquid, leaving 1/2-inch headspace.
f) Remove air bubbles and adjust headspace if needed. Wipe rims of jars with a dampened clean paper towel.

36. Pickled beets

Ingredients:
- 7 lbs. of 2- to 2-1/2-inch diameter beets
- 4 cups vinegar (5%)
- 1-1/2 teaspoons canning or pickling salt
- 2 cups sugar
- 2 cups water
- 2 cinnamon sticks
- 12 whole cloves
- 4 to 6 onions (2- to 2-1/2-inch diameter),

Yield: About 8 pints

Directions:

a) Trim of beet tops, leaving 1 inch of stem and roots to prevent bleeding of color.
b) Wash thoroughly. Sort for size. Cover similar sizes together with boiling water and cook until tender (about 25 to 30 minutes). Caution: Drain and discard liquid. Cool beets. Trim of roots and stems and slip of skins. Slice into 1/4-inch slices. Peel and thinly slice onions.
c) Combine vinegar, salt, sugar, and fresh water. Put spices in cheesecloth bag and add to vinegar mixture. Bring to a boil. Add beets and onions. Simmer 5 minutes. Remove spice bag.
d) Fill hot jars with beets and onions, leaving 1/2-inch headspace. Add hot vinegar solution, allowing 1/2-inch headspace.
e) Remove air bubbles and adjust headspace if needed. Wipe rims of jars with a dampened clean paper towel.

37. Pickled carrots

Ingredients:
- 2-3/4 lbs. peeled carrots
- 5-1/2 cups white vinegar (5%)
- 1 cup water
- 2 cups sugar
- 2 teaspoons canning salt
- 8 teaspoons mustard seed
- 4 teaspoons celery seed

Yield: About 4 pints

Directions:
- Wash and peel carrots. Cut into rounds that are approximately 1/2-inch thick.
- Combine vinegar, water, sugar and canning salt in an 8-quart Dutch oven or stockpot. Bring to a boil and boil 3 minutes. Add carrots and bring back to a boil. Then reduce heat to a simmer and heat until half-cooked (about 10 minutes).
- Meanwhile, place 2 teaspoons mustard seed and 1 tea-spoon celery seed into each empty hot pint jar. Fill jars with hot carrots, leaving 1-inch headspace. Fill with hot pickling liquid, leaving 1/2-inch headspace.
- Remove air bubbles and adjust headspace if needed. Wipe rims of jars with a dampened clean paper towel.

38. Pickled cauliflower/Brussels

Ingredients:
- 12 cups of 1- to 2-inch cauliflower flowerets or small Brussels sprouts
- 4 cups white vinegar (5%)
- 2 cups sugar
- 2 cups thinly sliced onions
- 1 cup diced sweet red peppers
- 2 Tablespoons mustard seed
- 1 Tablespoon celery seed
- 1 teaspoon turmeric
- 1 teaspoon hot red pepper lakes

Yield: About 9 half-pints

Directions:
a) Wash cauliflower flowerets or Brussels sprouts and boil in salt water (4 teaspoons canning salt per gallon of water) for 3 minutes for cauliflower and 4 minutes for Brussels sprouts. Drain and cool.
b) Combine vinegar, sugar, onion, diced red pepper, and spices in large saucepan. Bring to a boil and simmer 5 minutes.
c) Distribute onion and diced pepper among jars. Fill hot jars with pieces and pickling solution, leaving 1/2-inch head-space.
d) Remove air bubbles and adjust headspace if needed. Wipe rims of jars with a dampened clean paper towel.

39. Chayote and jicama slaw

Ingredients:
- 4 cups julienned jicama
- 4 cups julienned chayote
- 2 cups chopped red bell pepper
- 2 chopped hot peppers
- 2-1/2 cups water
- 2-1/2 cups cider vinegar (5%)
- 1/2 cup white sugar
- 3-1/2 teaspoons canning salt
- 1 teaspoon celery seed (optional)

Yield: About 6 half-pints

Directions:

a) Caution: Wear plastic or rubber gloves and do not touch your face while handling or cutting hot peppers. If you do not wear gloves, wash hands thoroughly with soap and water before touching your face or eyes.

b) Wash, peel and thinly julienne jicama and chayote, discarding the seed of the chayote. In an 8-quart Dutch oven or stockpot, combine all ingredients except chayote. Bring to a boil and boil for 5 minutes.

c) Reduce heat to simmering and add chayote. Bring back to a boil and then turn heat of. Fill hot solids into hot half-pint jars, leaving 1/2-inch headspace.

d) Cover with boiling cooking liquid, leaving 1/2-inch headspace.

e) Remove air bubbles and adjust headspace if needed. Wipe rims of jars with a dampened clean paper towel.

40. Bread-and-butter pickled jicama

Ingredients:
- 14 cups cubed jicama
- 3 cups thinly sliced onion
- 1 cup chopped red bell pepper
- 4 cups white vinegar (5%)
- 4-1/2 cups sugar
- 2 Tablespoons mustard seed
- 1 Tablespoon celery seed
- 1 teaspoon ground turmeric

Yield: About 6 pints

Directions:
a) Combine vinegar, sugar and spices in a 12-quart Dutch oven or large saucepot. Stir and bring to a boil. Stir in prepared jicama, onion slices, and red bell pepper. Return to a boil, reduce heat and simmer 5 minutes. Stir occasionally.
b) Fill hot solids into hot pint jars, leaving 1/2-inch headspace. Cover with boiling cooking liquid, leaving 1/2-inch headspace.
c) Remove air bubbles and adjust headspace if needed. Wipe rims of jars with a dampened clean paper towel.

41. Marinated whole mushrooms

Ingredients:
- 7 lbs. small whole mushrooms
- 1/2 cup bottled lemon juice
- 2 cups olive or salad oil
- 2-1/2 cups white vinegar (5%)
- 1 Tablespoon oregano leaves
- 1 Tablespoon dried basil leaves
- 1 Tablespoon canning or pickling salt
- 1/2 cup chopped onions
- 1/4 cup diced pimiento
- 2 cloves garlic, cut in quarters
- 25 black peppercorns

Yield: About 9 half-pints

Directions:
a) Select very fresh unopened mushrooms with caps less than 1-1/4 inch in diameter. Wash. Cut stems, leaving 1/4 inch attached to cap. Add lemon juice and water to cover. Bring to boil. Simmer 5 minutes. Drain mushrooms.
b) Mix olive oil, vinegar, oregano, basil, and salt in a saucepan. Stir in onions and pimiento and heat to boiling.
c) Place 1/4 garlic clove and 2-3 peppercorns in a half-pint jar. Fill hot jars with mushrooms and hot, well-mixed oil/vinegar solution, leaving 1/2-inch headspace.
d) Remove air bubbles and adjust headspace if needed. Wipe rims of jars with a dampened clean paper towel.

42. Pickled dilled okra

Ingredients
- 7 lbs. small okra pods
- 6 small hot peppers
- 4 teaspoons dill seed
- 8 to 9 garlic cloves
- 2/3 cup canning or pickling salt
- 6 cups water
- 6 cups vinegar (5%)

Yield: About 8 to 9 pints

Directions:
- Wash and trim okra. Fill hot jars firmly with whole okra, leaving 1/2-inch headspace. Place 1 garlic clove in each jar.
- Combine salt, hot peppers, dill seed, water, and vinegar in large saucepan and bring to a boil. Pour hot pickling solution over okra, leaving 1/2-inch headspace.
- Remove air bubbles and adjust headspace if needed. Wipe rims of jars with a dampened clean paper towel.

43. Pickled pearl onions

Ingredients:
- 8 cups peeled white pearl onions
- 5-1/2 cups white vinegar (5%)
- 1 cup water
- 2 teaspoons canning salt
- 2 cups sugar
- 8 teaspoons mustard seed
- 4 teaspoons celery seed

Yield: About 3 to 4 pints

Directions:
a) To peel onions, place a few at a time in a wire-mesh basket or strainer, dip in boiling water for 30 seconds, then remove and place in cold water for 30 seconds. Cut a 1/16th-inch slice from the root end, and then remove the peel and cut 1/16th-inch from the other end of the onion.
b) Combine vinegar, water, salt and sugar in an 8-quart Dutch oven or stockpot. Bring to a boil and boil 3 minutes.
c) Add peeled onions and bring back to a boil. Reduce heat to a simmer and heat until half-cooked (about 5 minutes).
d) Meanwhile, place 2 teaspoons mustard seed and 1 teaspoon celery seed into each empty hot pint jar. Fill with hot onions, leaving 1-inch headspace. Fill with hot pickling liquid, leaving 1/2-inch headspace.
e) Remove air bubbles and adjust headspace if needed. Wipe rims of jars with a dampened clean paper towel.

44. Marinated peppers

Ingredients:
- Bell, Hungarian, banana, or jalapeño
- 4 lbs. firm peppers
- 1 cup bottled lemon juice
- 2 cups white vinegar (5%)
- 1 Tablespoon oregano leaves
- 1 cup olive or salad oil
- 1/2 cup chopped onions
- 2 cloves garlic, quartered (optional)
- 2 Tablespoons prepared horseradish (optional)

Yield: About 9 half-pints

irections:

a) Select your favorite pepper. Caution: If you select hot peppers, wear plastic or rubber gloves and do not touch your face while handling or cutting hot peppers.

b) Wash, slash two to four slits in each pepper, and blanch in boiling water or blister skins on tough-skinned hot peppers using one of these two methods:

c) Oven or broiler method to blister skins – Place peppers in a hot oven (400°F) or under a broiler for 6 to 8 minutes until skins blister.

d) Range-top method to blister skins – Cover hot burner (either gas or electric) with heavy wire mesh.

e) Place peppers on burner for several minutes until skins blister.

f) After blistering skins, place peppers in a pan and cover with a damp cloth. (This will make peeling the peppers easier.) Cool several minutes; peel of skins. Flatten whole peppers.

g) Mix all remaining ingredients in a saucepan and heat to boiling. Place 1/4 garlic clove (optional) and 1/4 teaspoon salt in each hot half-pint jar or 1/2 teaspoon per pint. Fill hot jars with peppers. Add hot, well-mixed oil/pickling solution over peppers, leaving 1/2-inch headspace.

h) Remove air bubbles and adjust headspace if needed. Wipe rims of jars with a dampened clean paper towel.

45. **Pickled bell peppers**

Ingredients:
- 7 lbs. bell peppers
- 3-1/2 cups sugar
- 3 cups vinegar (5%)
- 3 cups water
- 9 cloves garlic
- 4-1/2 teaspoons canning or pickling salt

Yield: About 9 pints

Directions:
a) Wash peppers, cut into quarters, remove cores and seeds, and cut away any blemishes. Slice peppers in strips. Boil sugar, vinegar, and water for 1 minute.
b) Add peppers and bring to a boil. Place 1/2 clove of garlic and 1/4 teaspoon salt in each hot sterile half-pint jar; double the amounts for pint jars.
c) Add pepper strips and cover with hot vinegar mixture, leaving 1/2-inch

46. Pickled hot peppers

Ingredients:
- Hungarian, banana, chile, jalapeño
- 4 lbs. hot long red, green, or yellow peppers
- 3 lbs. sweet red and green peppers, mixed
- 5 cups vinegar (5%)
- 1 cup water
- 4 teaspoons canning or pickling salt
- 2 Tablespoons sugar
- 2 cloves garlic

Yield: About 9 pints

Directions:

a) Caution: Wear plastic or rubber gloves and do not touch your face while handling or cutting hot peppers. If you do not wear gloves, wash hands thoroughly with soap and water before touching your face or eyes.

b) Wash peppers. If small peppers are left whole, slash 2 to 4 slits in each. Quarter large peppers.

c) Blanch in boiling water or blister skins on tough-skinned hot peppers using one of these two methods:

d) Oven or broiler method to blister skins – Place peppers in a hot oven (400°F) or under a broiler for 6 to 8 minutes until skins blister.

e) Range-top method to blister skins – Cover hot burner (either gas or electric) with heavy wire mesh.

f) Place peppers on burner for several minutes until skins blister.

g) After blistering skins, place peppers in a pan and cover with a damp cloth. (This will make peeling the peppers easier.) Cool several minutes; peel of skins. Flatten small peppers. Quarter large peppers. Fill hot jars with peppers, leaving 1/2-inch headspace.

h) Combine and heat other ingredients to boiling and simmer 10 minutes. Remove garlic. Add hot pickling solution over peppers, leaving 1/2-inch headspace.

i) Remove air bubbles and adjust headspace if needed. Wipe rims of jars with a dampened clean paper towel.

47. Pickled jalapeño pepper rings

Ingredients:
- 3 lbs. jalapeño peppers
- 1-1/2 cups pickling lime
- 1-1/2 gallons water
- 7-1/2 cups cider vinegar (5%)
- 1-3/4 cups water
- 2-1/2 Tablespoons canning salt
- 3 Tablespoons celery seed
- 6 Tablespoons mustard seed

Yield: About 6 pint jars

Directions:
- Caution: Wear plastic or rubber gloves and do not touch your face while handling or cutting hot peppers.
- Wash peppers well and slice into 1/4-inch thick slices. Discard stem end.
- Mix 1-1/2 cups pickling lime with 1-1/2 gallons water in a stainless steel, glass or food grade plastic container. Avoid inhaling lime dust while mixing the lime-water solution.
- Soak pepper slices in the lime water, in refrigerator, for 18 hours, stirring occasionally (12 to 24 hours may be used). Drain lime solution from soaked pepper rings.
- Rinse peppers gently but thoroughly with water. Cover pepper rings with fresh cold water and soak, in refrigerator, 1 hour. Drain water from peppers. Repeat the rinsing, soaking and draining steps two more times. Drain thoroughly at the end.
- Place 1 tablespoon mustard seed and 1-1/2 teaspoons celery seed in the bottom of each hot pint jar. Pack drained pepper rings into the jars, leaving 1/2-inch headspace. Bring cider vinegar, 1-3/4 cups water and canning salt to a boil over high heat. Ladle boiling hot brine solution over pepper rings in jars, leaving 1/2-inch headspace.
- Remove air bubbles and adjust headspace if needed. Wipe rims of jars with a dampened clean paper towel.

48. Pickled yellow pepper rings

Ingredients:
- 2-1/2 to 3 lbs. yellow (banana) peppers
- 2 Tablespoons celery seed
- 4 Tablespoons mustard seed
- 5 cups cider vinegar (5%)
- 1-1/4 cups water
- 5 teaspoons canning salt

Yield: About 4 pint jars

Directions:
a) Wash peppers well and remove stem end; slice peppers into 1/4-inch thick rings. Place 1/2 tablespoon celery seed and 1 tablespoon mustard seed in the bottom of each empty hot pint jar.
b) Fill pepper rings into jars, leaving 1/2-inch head-space. In a 4-quart Dutch oven or saucepan, combine the cider vinegar, water and salt; heat to boiling. Cover pepper rings with boiling pickling liquid, leaving 1/2-inch headspace.
c) Remove air bubbles and adjust headspace if needed. Wipe rims of jars with a dampened clean paper towel.

49. Pickled sweet green tomatoes

Ingredients:
- 10 to 11 lbs. of green tomatoes
- 2 cups sliced onions
- 1/4 cup canning or pickling salt
- 3 cups brown sugar
- 4 cups vinegar (5%)
- 1 Tablespoon mustard seed
- 1 Tablespoon allspice
- 1 Tablespoon celery seed
- 1 Tablespoon whole cloves

Yield: About 9 pints

Directions:

a) Wash and slice tomatoes and onions. Place in bowl, sprinkle with 1/4 cup salt, and let stand 4 to 6 hours. Drain. Heat and stir sugar in vinegar until dissolved.

b) Tie mustard seed, allspice, celery seed, and cloves in a spice bag. Add to vinegar with tomatoes and onions. If needed, add minimum water to cover pieces. Bring to boil and simmer 30 minutes, stirring as needed to prevent burning. Tomatoes should be tender and transparent when properly cooked.

c) Remove spice bag. Fill hot jar with solids and cover with hot pickling solution, leaving 1/2-inch headspace.

d) Remove air bubbles and adjust headspace if needed. Wipe rims of jars with a dampened clean paper towel.

50. Pickled mixed vegetables

Ingredients:
- 4 lbs. of 4- to 5-inch pickling cucumbers
- 2 lbs. peeled and quartered small onions
- 4 cups cut celery (1-inch pieces)
- 2 cups peeled and cut carrots (1/2-inch pieces)
- 2 cups cut sweet red peppers (1/2-inch pieces)
- 2 cups cauliflower flowerets
- 5 cups white vinegar (5%)
- 1/4 cup prepared mustard
- 1/2 cup canning or pickling salt
- 3-1/2 cups sugar
- 3 Tablespoons celery seed
- 2 Tablespoons mustard seed
- 1/2 teaspoons whole cloves
- 1/2 teaspoons ground turmeric

Yield: About 10 pints

Directions:

a) Combine vegetables, cover with 2 inches of cubed or crushed ice, and refrigerate 3 to 4 hours. In 8-quart kettle, combine vinegar and mustard and mix well. Add salt, sugar, celery seed, mustard seed, cloves, turmeric. Bring to a boil. Drain vegetables and add to hot pickling solution.

b) Cover and slowly bring to boil. Drain vegetables but save pickling solution. Fill vegetables in hot sterile pint jars, or hot quarts, leaving 1/2-inch headspace. Add pickling solution, leaving 1/2-inch headspace.

c) Remove air bubbles and adjust headspace if needed. Wipe rims of jars with a dampened clean paper towel.

51. Pickled bread-and-butter zucchini

Ingredients:
- 16 cups fresh zucchini, sliced
- 4 cups onions, thinly sliced
- 1/2 cup canning or pickling salt
- 4 cups white vinegar (5%)
- 2 cups sugar
- 4 Tablespoons mustard seed
- 2 Tablespoons celery seed
- 2 teaspoons ground turmeric

Yield: About 8 to 9 pints

Directions:
c) Cover zucchini and onion slices with 1 inch of water and salt. Let stand 2 hours and drain thoroughly. Combine vinegar, sugar, and spices. Bring to a boil and add zucchini and onions. Simmer 5 minutes and ill hot jars with mixture and pickling solution, leaving 1/2-inch headspace.
d) Remove air bubbles and adjust headspace if needed. Wipe rims of jars with a dampened clean paper towel.

52. Chayote and pear relish

Ingredients:
- 3-1/2 cups peeled, cubed chayote
- 3-1/2 cups peeled, cubed Seckel pears
- 2 cups chopped red bell pepper
- 2 cups chopped yellow bell pepper
- 3 cups chopped onion
- 2 Serrano peppers, chopped
- 2-1/2 cups cider vinegar (5%)
- 1-1/2 cups water
- 1 cup white sugar
- 2 teaspoons canning salt
- 1 teaspoon ground allspice
- 1 teaspoon ground pumpkin pie spice

Yield: About 5 pint jars

Directions:
a) Wash, peel and cut chayote and pears into 1/2-inch cubes, discarding cores and seeds. Chop onions and peppers. Combine vinegar, water, sugar, salt and spices in a Dutch oven or large saucepot. Bring to a boil, stirring to dissolve sugar.
b) Add chopped onions and peppers; return to a boil and boil for 2 minutes, stirring occasionally.
c) Add cubed chayote and pears; return to the boiling point and turn off heat. Fill the hot solids into hot pint jars, leaving 1-inch headspace. Cover with boiling cooking liquid, leaving 1/2-inch head-space.
d) Remove air bubbles and adjust headspace if needed. Wipe rims of jars with a dampened clean paper towel.

53. Piccalilli

Ingredients:
- 6 cups chopped green tomatoes
- 1-1/2 cups chopped sweet red peppers
- 1-1/2 cups chopped green peppers
- 2-1/4 cups chopped onions
- 7-1/2 cups chopped cabbage
- 1/2 cup canning or pickling salt
- 3 Tablespoons whole mixed pickling spice
- 4-1/2 cups vinegar (5%)
- 3 cups brown sugar

Yield: About 9 half-pints

Directions:

a) Wash, chop, and combine vegetables with 1/2 cup salt. Cover with hot water and let stand 12 hours. Drain and press in a clean white cloth to remove all possible liquid. Tie spices loosely in a spice bag and add to combined vinegar and brown sugar and heat to a boil in a sauce pan.

b) Add vegetables and boil gently 30 minutes or until the volume of the mixture is reduced by one-half. Remove spice bag.

c) Fill hot sterile jars, with hot mixture, leaving 1/2-inch headspace.

d) Remove air bubbles and adjust headspace if needed. Wipe rims of jars with a dampened clean paper towel.

54. Pickle relish

Ingredients:
- 3 quarts chopped cucumbers
- 3 cups each of chopped sweet green and red peppers
- 1 cup chopped onions
- 3/4 cup canning or pickling salt
- 4 cups ice
- 8 cups water
- 2 cups sugar
- 4 teaspoons each of mustard seed, turmeric, whole allspice, and whole cloves
- 6 cups white vinegar (5%)

Yield: About 9 pints

Directions:
a) Add cucumbers, peppers, onions, salt, and ice to water and let stand 4 hours. Drain and re-cover vegetables with fresh ice water for another hour. Drain again.
b) Combine spices in a spice or cheesecloth bag. Add spices to sugar and vinegar. Heat to boiling and pour mixture over vegetables.
c) Cover and refrigerate 24 hours. Heat mixture to boiling and ill hot into hot jars, leaving 1/2-inch headspace.
d) Remove air bubbles and adjust headspace if needed. Wipe rims of jars with a dampened clean paper towel.

55. Pickled corn relish

Ingredients:
- 10 cups fresh whole kernel corn
- 2-1/2 cups diced sweet red peppers
- 2-1/2 cups diced sweet green peppers
- 2-1/2 cups chopped celery
- 1-1/4 cups diced onions
- 1-3/4 cups sugar
- 5 cups vinegar (5%)
- 2-1/2 Tablespoons canning or pickling salt
- 2-1/2 teaspoons celery seed
- 2-1/2 Tablespoons dry mustard
- 1-1/4 teaspoons turmeric

Yield: About 9 pints

Directions:
a) Boil ears of corn 5 minutes. Dip in cold water. Cut whole kernels from cob or use six 10-ounce frozen packages of corn.
b) Combine peppers, celery, onions, sugar, vinegar, salt, and celery seed in a saucepan.
c) Bring to boil and simmer 5 minutes, stirring occasionally. Mix mustard and turmeric in 1/2 cup of the simmered mixture. Add this mixture and corn to the hot mixture.
d) Simmer another 5 minutes. Fill hot jars with hot mixture, leaving 1/2-inch headspace.
e) Remove air bubbles and adjust headspace if needed. Wipe rims of jars with a dampened clean paper towel.

56. <u>Pickled green tomato relish</u>

Ingredients:
- 10 lbs. small, hard green tomatoes
- 1-1/2 lbs. red bell peppers
- 1-1/2 lbs. green bell peppers
- 2 lbs. onions
- 1/2 cup canning or pickling salt
- 1-quart water
- 4 cups sugar
- 1-quart vinegar (5%)
- 1/3 cup prepared yellow mustard
- 2 Tablespoons cornstarch

Yield: About 7 to 9 pints

Directions:
a) Wash and coarsely grate or chop tomatoes, peppers, and onions. Dissolve salt in water and pour over vegetables in large kettle.
b) Heat to boiling and simmer 5 minutes. Drain in colander. Return vegetables to kettle.
c) Add sugar, vinegar, mustard, and cornstarch. Stir to mix. Heat to boiling and simmer 5 minutes.
d) Fill hot sterile pint jars with hot relish, leaving 1/2-inch headspace.
e) Remove air bubbles and adjust headspace if needed. Wipe rims of jars with a dampened clean paper towel.

57. Pickled horseradish sauce

Ingredients:
- 2 cups (3/4 lb.) freshly grated horseradish
- 1 cup white vinegar (5%)
- 1/2 teaspoons canning or pickling salt
- 1/4 teaspoons powdered ascorbic acid

Directions:
a) The pungency of fresh horseradish fades within 1 to 2 months, even when refrigerated. Therefore, make only small quantities at a time.
b) Wash horseradish roots thoroughly and peel of brown outer skin. The peeled roots may be grated in a food processor or cut into small cubes and put through a food grinder.
c) Combine ingredients and ill into sterile jars, leaving 1/4-inch headspace.
d) Seal jars tightly and store in a refrigerator.

58. Pickled pepper-onion relish

Ingredients:
- 6 cups chopped onions
- 3 cups chopped sweet red peppers
- 3 cups chopped green peppers
- 1-1/2 cups sugar
- 6 cups vinegar (5%), preferably white distilled
- 2 Tablespoons canning or pickling salt

Yield: About 9 half-pints

Directions:

a) Wash and chop vegetables. Combine all ingredients and boil gently until mixture thickens and volume is reduced by one-half (about 30 minutes).

b) Fill hot sterile jars with hot relish, leaving 1/2-inch headspace, and seal tightly.

c) Store in refrigerator and use within one month.

59. Spicy jicama relish

Ingredients:
- 9 cups diced jicama
- 1 Tablespoon whole mixed pickling spice
- 1 two-inch stick cinnamon
- 8 cups white vinegar (5%)
- 4 cups sugar
- 2 teaspoons crushed red pepper
- 4 cups diced yellow bell pepper
- 4-1/2 cups diced red bell pepper
- 4 cups chopped onion
- 2 fresh hot peppers

Yield: About 7 pint jars

Directions:

a) Caution: Wear plastic or rubber gloves and do not touch your face while handling or cutting hot peppers. Wash, peel and trim jicama; dice.
b) Place pickling spice and cinnamon on a clean, double-layer, 6-inch-square piece of 100% cotton cheesecloth.
c) Bring corners together and tie with a clean string.
d) In a 4-quart Dutch oven or saucepot, combine pickling spice bag, vinegar, sugar, and crushed red pepper. Bring to boiling, stirring to dissolve sugar. Stir in diced jicama, sweet peppers, onion and fingerhots. Return mixture to boiling.
e) Reduce heat and simmer, covered, over medium-low heat about 25 minutes. Discard spice bag. Fill relish into hot pint jars, leaving 1/2-inch headspace. Cover with hot pickling liquid, leaving 1/2-inch headspace.
f) Remove air bubbles and adjust headspace if needed. Wipe rims of jars with a dampened clean paper towel.

60. Tangy tomatillo relish

Ingredients:
- 12 cups chopped tomatillos
- 3 cups chopped jicama
- 3 cups chopped onion
- 6 cups chopped plum-type tomatoes
- 1-1/2 cups chopped green bell pepper
- 1-1/2 cups chopped red bell pepper
- 1-1/2 cups chopped yellow bell pepper
- 1 cup canning salt
- 2 quarts water
- 6 Tablespoons whole mixed pickling spice
- 1 Tablespoon crushed red pepper flakes (optional)
- 6 cups sugar
- 6-1/2 cups cider vinegar (5%)

Yield: About 6 or 7 pints

Directions:
a) Remove husks from tomatillos and wash well. Peel jicama and onion. Wash all vegetables well before trimming and chopping.
b) Place chopped tomatillos, jicama, onion, tomatoes, and all bell peppers in a 4-quart Dutch oven or saucepot. Dissolve canning salt in water. Pour over prepared vegetables. Heat to boiling; simmer 5 minutes.
c) Drain thoroughly through a cheesecloth-lined strainer (until no more water drips through, about 15 to 20 minutes).
d) Place pickling spice and optional red pepper flakes on a clean, double-layer, 6 inch-square piece

61. No sugar added pickled beets

Ingredients:
- 7 lbs. of 2- to 2-1/2-inch diameter beets
- 4 to 6 onions (2- to 2-1/2-inch diameter), if desired
- 6 cups white vinegar (5 percent)
- 1-1/2 teaspoons canning or pickling salt
- 2 cups Splenda
- 3 cups water
- 2 cinnamon sticks
- 12 whole cloves

Yield: About 8 pints

Directions:
a) Trim of beet tops, leaving 1 inch of stem and roots to prevent bleeding of color. Wash thoroughly. Sort for size.
b) Cover similar sizes together with boiling water and cook until tender (about 25 to 30 minutes). Caution: Drain and discard liquid. Cool beets.
c) Trim of roots and stems and slip of skins. Slice into 1/4-inch slices. Peel, wash and thinly slice onions.
d) Combine vinegar, salt, Splenda®, and 3 cups fresh water in large Dutch oven. Tie cinnamon sticks and cloves in cheesecloth bag and add to vinegar mixture.
e) Bring to a boil. Add beets and onions. Simmer
f) 5 minutes. Remove spice bag. Fill hot beets and onion slices into hot pint jars, leaving 1/2-inch headspace. Cover with boiling vinegar solution, leaving 1/2-inch headspace.
g) Remove air bubbles and adjust headspace if needed. Wipe rims of jars with a dampened clean paper towel.

62. Sweet pickle cucumber

Ingredients:
- 3-1/2 lbs. of pickling cucumbers
- boiling water to cover sliced cucumbers
- 4 cups cider vinegar (5%)
- 1 cup water
- 3 cups Splenda®
- 1 Tablespoon canning salt
- 1 Tablespoon mustard seed
- 1 Tablespoon whole allspice
- 1 Tablespoon celery seed
- 4 one-inch cinnamon sticks

Yield: About 4 or 5 pint jars

Directions:
a) Wash cucumbers. Slice 1/16th-inch of the blossom ends and discard. Slice cucumbers into 1/4-inch thick slices. Pour boiling water over the cucumber slices and let stand 5 to 10 minutes.
b) Drain of the hot water and pour cold water over the cucumbers. Let cold water run continuously over the cucumber slices, or change water frequently until cucumbers are cooled. Drain slices well.
c) Mix vinegar, 1 cup water, Splenda® and all spices in a 10-quart Dutch oven or stockpot. Bring to a boil. Add drained cucumber slices carefully to the boiling liquid and return to a boil.
d) Place one cinnamon stick in each empty hot jar, if desired. Fill hot pickle slices into hot pint jars, leaving 1/2-inch headspace. Cover with boiling pickling brine, leaving 1/2-inch headspace.
e) Remove air bubbles and adjust headspace if needed. Wipe rims of jars with a dampened clean paper towel.

63. Sliced dill pickles

Ingredients:
- 4 lbs. (3- to 5-inch) pickling cucumbers
- 6 cups vinegar (5%)
- 6 cups sugar
- 2 Tablespoons canning or pickling salt
- 1-1/2 teaspoons celery seed
- 1-1/2 teaspoons mustard seed
- 2 large onions, thinly sliced
- 8 heads fresh dill

Yield: About 8 pints

Directions:

a) Wash cucumbers. Cut 1/16-inch slice of blossom end and discard. Cut cucumbers in 1/4-inch slices. Combine vinegar, sugar, salt, celery, and mustard seeds in large saucepan. Bring mixture to boiling.

b) Place 2 slices of onion and 1/2 dill head on bottom of each hot pint jar. Fill hot jars with cucumber slices, leaving 1/2-inch headspace.

c) Add 1 slice of onion and 1/2 dill head on top. Pour hot pickling solution over cucumbers, leaving 1/4-inch headspace.

d) Remove air bubbles and adjust headspace if needed. Wipe rims of jars with a dampened clean paper towel.

64. Sliced sweet pickles

Ingredients:
- 4 lbs. (3- to 4-inch) pickling cucumbers

Brining solution:
- 1-quart distilled white vinegar (5%)
- 1 Tablespoon canning or pickling salt
- 1 Tablespoon mustard seed
- 1/2 cup sugar

Canning syrup:
- 1-2/3 cups distilled white vinegar (5%)
- 3 cups sugar
- 1 Tablespoon whole allspice
- 2-1/4 teaspoons celery seed

Yield: About 4 to 5 pints

Directions:
- Wash cucumbers and cut 1/16 inch of blossom end, and discard. Cut cucumbers into 1/4-inch slices. Combine all ingredients for canning syrup in a saucepan and bring to boiling. Keep syrup hot until used.
- In a large kettle, mix the ingredients for the brining solution. Add the cut cucumbers, cover, and simmer until the cucumbers change color from bright to dull green (about 5 to 7 minutes). Drain the cucumber slices.
- Fill hot jars, and cover with hot canning syrup leaving 1/2-inch headspace.
- Remove air bubbles and adjust headspace if needed. Wipe rims of jars with a dampened clean paper towel.

65. Lemon & Dill Kraut

Ingredients:
- 1 head firm white cabbage, finely sliced
- 2 to 3 teaspoons sea salt (1.5%)
- 2 tablespoons lemon juice
- 1 tablespoon dried dill
- 2 -3 cloves garlic, finely grated

Directions:
a) Wash your cabbage and reserve one of the outer leaves to tuck in top of your kraut.
b) Cut the cabbage in quarters, remove the core, and shred finely. Follow the directions above for normal sauerkraut, adding the lemon juice and the dried dill with the salt.
c) Squeeze and massage the cabbage until it is glistening and there is a small pool of liquid in the bottom of the bowl, then mix in the garlic.

66. Chinese Kimchi

Ingredients:
- 1 head of napa or Chinese cabbage, chopped
- 3 carrots, grated
- 1 large daikon radish, grated or a cup of small red radishes, finely sliced
- 1 large onion, chopped
- 1/4 cup of dulse or nori seaweed flakes
- 1 tablespoon chile pepper flakes
- 1 tablespoon minced garlic
- 1 tablespoon minced fresh ginger
- 1 tablespoon sesame seeds
- 1 tablespoon sugar
- 2 teaspoons good quality sea salt
- 1 teaspoon of fish sauce

Directions:

a) Simply mix all the ingredients together in a large bowl and let it sit for 30 minutes.
b) Pack the mixture into a large glass mason jar or 2 smaller jars. Press it down firmly.
c) Top with a water filled Ziploc bag to keep oxygen out and keep the veggies submerged under the brine.
d) Put the lid on loosely and set aside to ferment for at least 3 days. Taste it after 3 days and decide whether it tastes sour enough. It's a matter of personal taste so just keep trying it until you like it!
e) Once you are happy with the flavour you can store the kimchi in the fridge where it will keep happily for months, if it lasts that long!!

.

67. **Fermented Carrot Sticks**

Ingredients:
- 6 organic carrots, washed and cut into sticks
- 2 % brine solution (20g sea salt dissolved in 1 litre filtered water)
- Few garlic cloves, lemon slices, black peppercorns, bay leaves or dill

Directions:

a) Pack the carrots tightly into a clean 1 litre glass jar, along with any other seasoning from the ingredients list. Pour the brine over to within 2.5 cm of the top of the jar.

b) If the carrots are floating above the level of liquid, then you can use a Ziploc bag filled with brine to weigh them down and keep them safely submerged.

c) Leave to ferment at room temperature, out of direct sunlight, for at least a week, but preferably two weeks. The brine will start to look cloudy which indicates fermentation is proceeding normally. You should also see some bubbles if you gently shake the jar.

d) Once you are happy with the flavour and texture then move them to the fridge, where they will keep happily for a few months!

68. Carrots with an Indian Twist

(Makes 1 litre jar)

Ingredients:
- 1 kg carrots, peeled and grated
- 1 knob fresh ginger, peeled and grated
- 2 tsp chili flakes
- 2 tsp fenugreek
- 2 tsp mustard seed
- 1 tsp ground turmeric
- 1 tablespoon sea salt

Directions:
a) Place the carrots in a bowl and sprinkle with the sea salt.
b) Squeeze and massage the mixture to release some brine. The carrots should start to wilt and become wet.
c) Add the spices and mix together using a wooden spoon, not your hands or they will be stained orange by the turmeric!
d) Pack the mixture into a clean 1 litre glass jar, pressing each handful down firmly to ensure no air is trapped. Leave 2.5cm headspace at the top of the jar and make sure the carrots are completely submerged under the brine.
e) Close the lid and allow to ferment for 5 to 7 days at room temperature.
f) Store the jar in the fridge and use within 6 months.

69. Radish Bombs

(Makes 1 litre jar)

Ingredients:
- 400g radishes, tops trimmed
- 1 or 2 tsp pickling spice or fennel
- 15g/1 tablespoon sea salt
- 10g/2 tsp caster sugar
- 1 litre filtered water
- 1 red onion sliced or 5 spring onions
- 3 slices fresh ginger
- 2 or 3 large slices of lemon
- 3 or 4 garlic cloves, smashed
- 1 tsp or more dried chili flakes, depending how hot you like it

Directions:

a) Make the brine by dissolving the sea salt and sugar in a jug. Wash your glass jar in hot soapy water and rinse it well to remove any soap residues.

b) Put the spices in the bottom of the jar, then add the vegetables, finishing with the lemon slices on top. Pour the brine over until everything is completely submerged. Cover with a large cabbage leaf or Ziploc bag filled with extra brine to keep everything under the brine.

c) Loosely close the jar and leave somewhere cool and out of direct sunlight for 7 to 12 days. I tend to put mine in the garage since the sulphurous pong can be quite overpowering and you may get complaints from family members!

d) Taste them after 7 days and if they are sour enough for you then transfer them to the fridge where they will keep for around 6 months.

e) If not sour enough then leave them another 4 or 5 days.

f) Keep any excess brine and use it in salad dressings, its teeming with probiotics!!

MASON JAR DESSERT

70. Cadbury Egg Trifles

Makes: 4

INGREDIENTS:
- 3.4-ounce box of vanilla pudding
- 1 cup cold milk
- 1 can of sweetened condensed milk
- 8-ounce tub Cool whip, divided
- 2 cups milk chocolate chips
- 1 cup heavy cream
- 3 cups chopped Oreos
- Cadbury creme eggs, for garnish

INSTRUCTIONS:
MAKE PUDDING:
d) In a large bowl, whisk together the pudding mix, milk, and sweetened condensed milk. Let set for 5 minutes, stirring often, until the mixture has thickened.
MAKE GANACHE:
e) In a small saucepan over medium heat, bring heavy cream to a low simmer. Add milk chocolate chips to a medium bowl, then pour hot heavy cream on top. Let sit for 3 minutes, then whisk until the chocolate has melted and the mixture is smooth. Let cool to room temperature.
ASSEMBLE TRIFLES:
f) Add an even layer of chopped Oreos into the bottoms of 4 large mason jars. Top with an even layer of pudding mixture, spread milk chocolate ganache over the pudding then dollop Cool Whip on top. Repeat to make another layer of each ingredient.
g) Refrigerate until ready to serve.

71. Raw Parfait with Spirulina Milk

Makes: 1

INGREDIENTS:
DRY
- ½ cup oats
- 1 tablespoon apple, dried
- 1 tablespoon almonds, activated
- 1 tablespoon sweet cacao nibs
- 1 tablespoon apricots, dried, finely chopped
- ½ teaspoons vanilla powder
- 1 tablespoon maca powder

LIQUID
- 1 cup, cashew milk
- 1 tablespoon spirulina powder
- 2 Tablespoons pumpkin seeds, ground

INSTRUCTIONS:
a) In a mason jar add and layer the oats, apples, almonds, and apricots and top with cacao nibs.
b) Then place cashew milk, spirulina, and pumpkin seeds into a blender and pulse on high for one minute.
c) Pour the finished milk over the dry ingredients and enjoy.

72. Blueberry lemon cheesecake oats

INGREDIENTS:
- ¼ cup non-fat Greek yogurt
- 2 tablespoons blueberry yogurt
- ¼ cup blueberries
- 1 teaspoon grated lemon zest
- 1 teaspoon honey

INSTRUCTIONS:
a) Combine the oats and milk in a 16-ounce mason jar; top with desired toppings.
b) Refrigerate overnight or up to 3 days; serve cold.

73. **Lime Flax Pudding**

Makes: 1 serving

INGREDIENTS:
- 1 ¼ cups 2% milk
- 1 cup 2% plain Greek yogurt
- ½ cup flax seeds
- 2 tablespoons honey
- 2 tablespoons sugar
- 2 teaspoons lime zest
- 2 tablespoons freshly squeezed lime juice
- 1 teaspoon vanilla extract
- 1 cup chopped strawberries and blueberries
- ½ cup diced mango and ½ cup diced kiwi

INSTRUCTIONS:
a) In a large bowl, whisk together the milk, yogurt, flax seeds, honey, sugar, lime zest, lime juice, vanilla, and salt until well combined.
b) Divide the mixture evenly into four mason jars.
c) Cover and refrigerate overnight, or for up to 5 days.
d) Serve cold, topped with strawberries, mango, kiwi, and blueberries.

74. Individual Key Lime Cheesecakes

INGREDIENTS

For the crust
- 1 1/4 cups (125 g) ground gluten-free shortbread cookies (such as Pamela's brand)
- 1 1/2 teaspoons brown sugar
- 2 tablespoons (28 g) unsalted butter, melted Pinch of salt

For the cheesecake
- 8 ounces (227 g) cream cheese, at room temperature
- 1 tablespoon (8 g) cornstarch
- 1/3 cup (65 g) granulated sugar
- Pinch of salt
- 1 tablespoon (15 ml) Key lime juice
- 1/4 cup (60 g) sour cream, at room temperature
- 1 teaspoon gluten-free vanilla extract
- 1 tablespoon (6 g) finely grated Key lime zest, plus more for garnishing
- 1 large egg, at room temperature 1 1/2 cups (355 ml) water Whipped cream, for garnishing

Crust

a) Lightly spray the insides of six 4-ounce (115 g) mason jars with nonstick cooking spray.

b) In a small bowl, mix together the crushed cookies, brown sugar, butter, and salt. Divide the cookie mixture evenly among the mason jars. Gently press the cookie crust against the bottom of the glasses.

Cheesecake

c) In a medium mixing bowl, beat the cream cheese with a hand mixer on low speed, until smooth. In a small mixing bowl, combine the cornstarch, granulated sugar, and salt. Add the sugar mixture to the cream cheese and beat until just incorporated. Scrape down the sides of the bowl with a spatula.

d) Add the lime juice, sour cream, vanilla, and lime zest to the cream cheese mixture. Beat until it just comes together. Add the egg; stir until just combined. Do not overmix.
e) Divide the cheesecake batter equally among the jars. Lightly tap the jars against the counter to release any large air bubbles.
f) Add the water to the bottom of the inner pot. Place a trivet inside the pot. Place the filled jars on the trivet, being careful the sides of the jars don't touch each other or the sides of the pot. You should be able to fit five around the edges and have space for one jar in the middle. Lightly place a large piece of foil over all the jars.
g) Close and lock the lid, making sure the steam release knob is in the sealing position. Cook on high pressure for 4 minutes. When the cook time is finished, allow a natural release for 10 minutes, then move the knob to the venting position and release any remaining steam. When the float pin drops, unlock the lid and open it carefully. Press Cancel.
h) Remove the foil and absorb any condensation on the surface of the cheesecakes by gently blotting with a paper towel. Allow the cheesecakes to cool inside the pot for 30 minutes, then remove to a cooling rack and let cool until they reach room temperature. Cover the cheesecakes with plastic wrap and place in the refrigerator for at least 6 to 8 hours, preferably overnight.
i) Serve garnished with whipped cream and additional lime zest.

Yield: 6 individual cheesecakes

75. Coconut Raspberry Curd

Servings 4

Ingredients
- 4 ounces coconut oil, softened
- 3/4 cup Swerve
- 4 egg yolks, beaten
- 1/2 cup blueberries
- 1 teaspoon grated lemon zest
- 1/2 teaspoon vanilla extract
- 1/2 teaspoon star anise, ground

Directions
1. Blend the coconut oil and Swerve in a food processor.
2. Gradually mix in the eggs; continue to blend for 1 minute longer.
3. Now, add blueberries, lemon zest, vanilla, and star anise. Divide the mixture among four Mason jars and cover them with lids.
4. Add 1 ½ cups of water and a metal rack to the Instant Pot. Now, lower your jars onto the rack.
5. Secure the lid. Choose "Manual" mode and High pressure; cook for 15 minutes. Once cooking is complete, use a natural pressure release; carefully remove the lid. Serve
6. Place in your refrigerator until ready to serve. Bon appétit!

76. Crème with Almond and Chocolate

Servings 4

Ingredients
- 2 cups heavy whipping cream
- 1/2 cup water
- 4 eggs
- 1/3 cup Swerve
- 1 teaspoon almond extract
- 1 teaspoon vanilla extract
- 1/3 cup almonds, ground
- 2 tablespoons coconut oil, room temperature
- 4 tablespoons cacao powder
- 2 tablespoons gelatin

Directions
1. Start by adding 1 ½ cups of water and a metal rack to your Instant Pot.
2. Blend the cream, water, eggs, Swerve, almond extract, vanilla extract and almonds in your food processor.
3. Add the remaining ingredients and process for a minute longer.
4. Divide the mixture between four Mason jars; cover your jars with lids. Lower the jars onto the rack.
5. Secure the lid. Choose "Manual" mode and High pressure; cook for 7 minutes. Once cooking is complete, use a natural pressure release; carefully remove the lid. Bon appétit!

77. Classic Holiday Custard

Preparation Time: 20 minutes + chilling time
Servings 4
Nutritional Values per serving: 201 Calories; 17.7g Fat; 6.2g Total Carbs; 4.2g Protein; 1.2g Sugars

Ingredients
- 5 egg yolks
- 1/3 cup coconut milk, unsweetened
- 1/2 teaspoon vanilla extract
- 1 teaspoon monk fruit powder
- 1 tablespoon butterscotch flavoring
- 1/2 stick butter, melted

Directions
1. Blend the egg yolks with coconut milk, vanilla extract, monk fruit powder, and butterscotch flavoring.
2. Then, stir in the butter; stir until everything is well incorporated. Divide the mixture among four Mason jars and cover them with lids.
3. Add 1 ½ cups of water and a metal rack to the Instant Pot. Now, lower your jars onto the rack.
4. Secure the lid. Choose "Manual" mode and Low pressure; cook for 15 minutes. Once cooking is complete, use a natural pressure release; carefully remove the lid. Serve
5. Place in your refrigerator until ready to serve. Bon appétit!

78. Chocolate Cream

Preparation Time: 25 MIN
Serving: 4
Ingredients:
- 2 heavy cream
- ¼ cup unsweetened dark chocolate, chopped
- 3 eggs
- 1 tsp orange zest
- 1 tsp stevia powder
- 1 tsp vanilla extract
- ½ tsp salt

Directions:
1. Plug in your instant pot and press the 'Saute' button. Add heavy cream, chopped chocolate, stevia powder, vanilla extract, orange zest, and salt. Stir well and simmer until the chocolate has completely melted. Press the 'Cancel' button and crack eggs, one at the time, stirring constantly. Remove from the instant pot.
2. Transfer the mixture to 4 mason jars with loose lids.
3. Pour 2 cups of water in your instant pot and set the trivet in the stainless steel insert. Add jars and seal the lid.
4. Set the steam release handle and press the 'Manual' button. Set the timer for 10 minutes.
5. When done, perform a quick release by moving the steam valve to the 'Venting' position.
6. Open the lid and remove the jars. Chill to a room temperature and then transfer to the refrigerator.
7. Top with some whipped cream before serving.

79. <u>Tzatziki</u>

Makes about 1½ to 2 cups

Ingredients:
- 1 cup raw, unsalted cashews
- ½ cup filtered water
- 1 probiotic capsule or ¼ teaspoon probiotic powder
- Juice from 1 lemon
- 1 garlic clove, minced
- 2 tablespoons minced onion
- 1 teaspoon unrefined sea salt
- One 3-inch piece of a medium cucumber

a) In a small to medium glass bowl, combine the cashews and water. Empty the contents of the probiotic capsule (discarding the empty capsule shell) or probiotic powder into the cashew mixture, and stir to combine. Cover and set aside for twenty-four hours.

b) In a blender, combine the cashew mixture with the lemon juice, garlic, onion, and salt, and blend until smooth and creamy; return the mixture to the bowl. Grate the cucumber, add it to the cashew mixture, and stir until combined. Store, covered, in the refrigerator for up to three days.

c) When ready to serve, garnish with cucumber slices and/or slivers, if desired.

80. Creamy French Onion Dip

Makes about 2½ cups

Ingredients:
- 2 cups raw, unsalted cashews
- 1½ cups filtered water
- 2 probiotic capsules or ½ teaspoon probiotic powder
- Juice from ½ lemon
- 2 tablespoons minced green onion
- 2 tablespoons minced fresh parsley
- About 1 teaspoon unrefined sea salt, or to taste
- Chives or spring onions for garnish (optional)

Directions:

a) In a small to medium glass bowl, combine the cashews and water.

b) Empty the contents of the probiotic capsules (discarding the empty capsule shells) or probiotic powder into the cashews, and stir to mix.

c) Cover and allow the mixture to culture for twenty-four to forty-eight hours.

d) When ready to serve, garnish with chives or spring onions, if desired.

81. Green Salad with Peaches & Chèvre

Serves 2 to 4

Ingredients:

Salad
- 1 small package mixed greens
- 2 to 3 fresh peaches, pitted and halved
- 1 tablespoon extra-virgin olive oil
- 1-inch round Chèvre

Dressing
- ¾ cup extra-virgin olive oil
- ⅓ cup apple cider vinegar
- ½ teaspoon unrefined sea salt
- ½ teaspoon dried basil
- ½ teaspoon dried thyme
- 1 teaspoon pure maple syrup or agave nectar

Preheat your barbecue to 300 to 350ºF, or heat a cast-iron grill pan on your stovetop over low to medium heat.

Wash and dry the mesclun greens, and place in a large bowl; set aside.

Brush the peach halves with olive oil, and place flat side down on the barbecue or grill pan. Grill for about 3 minutes, or until peaches are soft but not mushy. Remove the peaches from the grill, turn off the heat, and set aside.

Cut the Chèvre into discs, and set aside.

In a blender, combine all dressing ingredients, and blend until smooth. Pour your desired amount of dressing over the mixed greens, and toss the salad until it is well coated. Store any leftover dressing in a covered jar for up to one week.

Top the salad with the Chèvre discs and grilled peach halves, and serve in large bowls or on plates.

82. Coconut Cream Cheese

Ingredients:
- One 13.5-ounce can coconut milk
- 1 probiotic capsule or ¼ teaspoon probiotic powder
- 1 to 2 teaspoons pure maple syrup
- 1 teaspoon vanilla powder or pure vanilla extract
- 1 teaspoon lemon zest (optional)

Directions:

a) Open the can of coconut milk. If the coconut cream and water have already separated, scoop off the thick cream into a small bowl.

b) If it has not separated, in a small bowl simply mix both the coconut cream and coconut water together until smooth.

c) Add the contents of the probiotic capsule (discarding the empty capsule shell) or probiotic powder, and mix together.

d) Cover with a lid or cloth, and allow it to sit undisturbed for eight to ten hours in a warm setting (approximately 110 to 115ºF or 43 to 46ºC, but don't worry if it's not quite within that range).

e) After it has cultured, refrigerate for at least one to two hours. If the coconut cream and water have separated, scoop off the thickened coconut cream for use.

f) Add the maple syrup, vanilla powder or extract, and lemon zest if desired. Stir together until smooth. Use immediately as an icing for cakes, cupcakes, or other baked goods.

g) Lasts about one week, covered, in the fridge.

83. Pear Crêpes with Macadamia Cheese

Makes 8 large crêpes

Ingredients:

Crêpes
- 2 tablespoons olive oil, plus more for oiling frying pan
- 1½ cups all-purpose gluten-free flour (I use Bob's Red Mill xanthan-free flour)
- 1½ cups almond milk
- 2 tablespoons finely ground flaxseed whisked into 6 tablespoons water
- 1 teaspoon baking soda
- Pinch unrefined sea salt

Cardamom Pear Topping
- 4 medium pears, cored and sliced
- Pinch ground cardamom
- ½ cup filtered water, divided
- 2 tablespoons organic cane sugar
- 1 tablespoon tapioca flour

Cream Cheese Topping
- Macadamia Cream Cheese

a) For the crêpe batter, in a large bowl combine the 2 tablespoons oil, flour, almond milk, flaxseed-water mixture, baking soda, and salt; whisk together.

b) In a large frying pan over medium heat, add enough oil to grease the entire bottom of the pan, and pour enough crêpe batter to thinly coat the pan. Cook for approximately 1 minute or until the bubbles disappear, and flip. Repeat with the remaining batter until the batter is all used up.

c) For the topping, in a medium frying pan over low to medium heat, add the pears, cardamom, and ¼ cup of the water. Cook for approximately 5 minutes or until the pears are slightly softened. In a small glass bowl, combine the remaining ¼ cup of water, sugar, and tapioca until they are well mixed.

d) Add the sugar-tapioca mixture to the pears, stirring constantly. Allow to cook for another minute or until the sauce has thickened.
e) Top each crêpe with ⅛ of the pear mixture and ⅛ of the macadamia cream cheese. Serve immediately.

84. Gingerbread Cookie Ice Cream Sandwiches

Makes about 24 cookies or 12 ice cream sandwiches
Ingredients:
- ½ cup coconut oil
- ½ cup coconut sugar
- ¼ cup molasses
- 1 tablespoon finely ground flaxseed whisked into 3 tablespoons water
- 1 cup brown rice flour
- 1 cup millet flour
- 1½ teaspoons baking soda
- 2 teaspoons ground ginger
- 1 teaspoon ground cinnamon
- ¼ teaspoon ground nutmeg
- Cultured Vanilla Ice Cream

a) Preheat your oven to 350ºF.
b) In a mixer, combine the oil and sugar, and begin mixing. While they're still blending, add the molasses, flaxseed-water mixture, brown rice flour, millet flour, baking soda, ginger, cinnamon, and nutmeg, and continue to mix until the mixture forms a soft, pliable dough.
c) Form the dough into balls approximately 1½ inches in diameter, or the size of a walnut. Press them firmly with the palm of your hand onto a parchment-lined baking sheet to form 2-inch disks, leaving space between the cookies for them to spread. Bake for 8 minutes or until they are firm but not hard. Let cool on wire racks.
d) Once the gingerbread cookies have cooled, spoon the cultured vanilla ice cream onto one of the cookies, and press another cookie onto it to form a sandwich. Repeat for the remaining cookies. Freeze or serve immediately. If freezing, allow the ice cream sandwiches to sit at room temperature for about 10 minutes before serving.

85. Cultured Vanilla Ice Cream

Ingredients:
- 1 cup raw, unsalted cashews
- 2 cups almond milk
- 1 probiotic capsule or ¼ teaspoon probiotic powder
- 5 large fresh Medjool dates, pitted
- 1 teaspoon vanilla powder

Directions:
a) In a small bowl, combine the cashews and 1 cup of milk; add the contents of the probiotic capsule (discarding the empty capsule shell) or probiotic powder, and mix well.
b) Cover and let sit for eight to twelve hours, depending on your taste preference; longer fermentation times create a tangier flavor.
c) In a blender, combine the cashew mixture, dates, and vanilla powder, and blend until smooth. Pour into an ice cream machine, and follow the manufacturer's directions to process into ice cream (usually 20 to 25 minutes).

86. Pumpkin Pie Ice Cream

Makes about 1 quart/liter

Ingredients:
- ½ cup raw, unsalted cashews
- ¼ cup filtered water
- 2 probiotic capsules, or ½ teaspoon probiotic powder
- 2 cups almond milk
- 2 cups cooked squash
- 7 fresh Medjool dates, pitted
- 1½ teaspoons ground cinnamon
- ½ teaspoon ground ginger
- ½ teaspoon ground cloves
- ⅛ teaspoon nutmeg

Directions:

a) In a small bowl, mix the cashews and water; add the contents of the probiotic capsule (discarding the empty capsule shell) or probiotic powder, and mix well. Cover and let sit for twelve hours.

b) In a blender, combine the cashew mixture with the milk, squash, dates, cinnamon, ginger. cloves, and nutmeg, and blend until the mixture is smooth. Pour it into an ice cream maker, and follow the manufacturer's instructions. Serve immediately.

87. Black Cherry Ice Cream

Makes about 1 quart/liter

Ingredients:
- 1 cup raw, unsalted cashews
- 1 cup filtered water
- 1 probiotic capsule or ¼ teaspoon probiotic powder
- 2 cups fresh black cherries, pitted and stems removed (if using frozen cherries, allow to thaw before using), plus a few more for garnish (optional)
- 1¼ cup almond milk
- 4 fresh medjool dates, pitted

Directions:
a) In a medium bowl, soak cashews in the water for eight hours or overnight.
b) Pour the cashews and water into a blender, and blend until the mixture is smooth and creamy. Pour it into a small glass dish with a lid. Empty the probiotic capsule (discarding the empty capsule shell) or probiotic powder into the cashew mixture, and stir together. Cover it with a lid or clean cloth, and allow it to ferment for eight to twelve hours.
c) In a blender or food processor, combine the cashew mixture with the cherries, milk, and dates, and blend until smooth. Pour the mixture into an ice cream maker, and follow the manufacturer's directions to process into ice cream. Garnish with additional cherries if desired, and serve immediately.

88. Orange Creamsicle Cheesecake

Makes one 12-inch cheesecake

Ingredients:

Crust
- 1 cup raw, unsalted almonds
- 3 fresh Medjool dates, pitted
- 1 tablespoon coconut oil
- Pinch unrefined sea salt

Filling
- 2 cups raw, unsalted cashews
- 1 cup filtered water
- 1 probiotic capsule or ¼ teaspoon probiotic powder
- 3 cups orange juice
- 2 tablespoons pure maple syrup
- 1 teaspoon vanilla powder
- 1 cup coconut oil
- ¼ cup plus 1 tablespoon lecithin (5 tablespoons)
- Thin slices of orange, with peel, for garnish (optional)

Directions:

a) For the crust, in a food processor, combine all crust ingredients, and blend until finely chopped. Transfer to a 12-inch springform pan, and press over the bottom surface of the pan until it is firm.

b) For the filling, in a medium bowl, combine the cashews, water, and the contents of the probiotic capsule (discarding the empty capsule shell) or probiotic powder; stir until combined. Cover with a lid or clean cloth, and let sit for twelve to twenty-four hours to culture.

c) In a blender, combine the cashew mixture with the orange juice, maple syrup, vanilla powder, oil, and lecithin, and blend until smooth.

d) Pour the mixture over the crust. Refrigerate for four to six hours, or until set. Garnish with orange slices if desired, and serve. The cheesecake lasts approximately four days in the refrigerator in a covered container.

89. Pomegranate Cheesecake

Makes one 12-inch cheesecake

Ingredients:

Crust
- 1 cup raw, unsalted hazelnuts
- 4 fresh Medjool dates, pitted
- 1 tablespoon coconut oil
- Pinch unrefined sea salt

Filling
- 2 cups raw, unsalted cashews
- 1 cup filtered water
- 1 probiotic capsule or ¼ teaspoon probiotic powder
- 3 cups pomegranate juice
- 2 tablespoons pure maple syrup or agave nectar
- 1 teaspoon vanilla powder
- 1 cup coconut oil
- ¼ cup plus 2 tablespoons lecithin (6 tablespoons)
- Fresh pomegranate arils (seeds) to garnish (optional)

Directions:

a) For the crust, in a food processor, combine all crust ingredients, and blend until finely chopped. Transfer to a 12-inch springform pan, and press over the bottom surface of the pan until it is firm.

b) For the filling, in a medium bowl, combine the cashews, water, and the contents of the probiotic capsule (discarding the empty capsule shell) or probiotic powder. Stir the mixture until it is combined. Cover with a lid or clean cloth, and let sit for twelve to twenty-four hours to culture.

c) In a blender, combine the cashew mixture with the pomegranate juice, maple syrup or agave nectar, vanilla powder, oil, and lecithin, and blend until smooth.

d) Pour the mixture over the crust. Refrigerate for four to six hours, or until set. Top with fresh pomegranate arils if desired. Serve.

e) The cheesecake lasts approximately four days in the refrigerator in a covered container.

90. Blackberry Cheesecake

Makes one 12-inch cheesecake

Ingredients:

Crust
- 1 cup raw, unsalted almonds
- 3 fresh Medjool dates, pitted
- 1 tablespoon coconut oil
- Pinch unrefined sea salt

Filling
- 2 cups raw, unsalted cashews
- 1 cup filtered water
- 1 probiotic capsule or ¼ teaspoon probiotic powder
- ¼ cup plus 1 tablespoon pure maple syrup (5 tablespoons)
- 1 teaspoon vanilla powder
- ½ cup coconut oil
- ½ cup lecithin
- 2 cups almond milk

Directions:

a) 2½ cups fresh blackberries (if using frozen, allow them to thaw before making the cheesecake), plus more for garnish.
b) For the crust, in a food processor, combine all crust ingredients, and blend until finely chopped. Transfer to a 12-inch springform pan, and press over the bottom surface of the pan until it is firm.
c) For the filling, in a medium bowl, combine the cashews, water, and the contents of the probiotic capsule (discarding the empty capsule shell) or probiotic powder; stir the mixture until it is combined. Cover with a lid or clean cloth, and let sit for twenty-four to forty-eight hours to culture.
d) In a blender, combine the cashew mixture with the maple syrup, vanilla powder, oil, lecithin, and milk, and blend until smooth. Add the blackberries, and blend until smooth.
e) Pour the mixture over the crust. Refrigerate for four to six hours, or until set. Garnish with additional blackberries, if desired, and serve. The cheesecake lasts approximately four days in the refrigerator in a covered container.

91. Sweet Vanilla Peaches

Makes about 5 cups

Ingredients:
- 5 medium peaches, pitted and coarsely chopped (about 5 cups chopped)
- ½ teaspoon vanilla powder
- ½ teaspoon cardamom powder (optional)
- 1 tablespoon pure maple syrup
- 2 tablespoons whey

Directions:
a) In a large bowl, combine all the ingredients and mix well. Scoop the mixture into a 1-quart mason jar, cover, and let sit for twelve hours.
b) Refrigerate, where it should keep for four days.

MASON JAR DRINKS

92. Lemon and Cucumber Cooler

SERVINGS 2 drinks

Ingredients
- Crushed ice
- 1 small Kirby cucumber
- ½ small lemon
- 2 teaspoons sugar
- 1/2 teaspoons of freshly grated ginger
- Seltzer water
- Zubrowka Bison Grass Vodka

Directions

a) Fill both mason jars with crushed ice to 34% capacity. Cucumber should be sliced into thin rounds. Divide the mixture between the two mason jars. To each mason jar, add 1 teaspoon of sugar.

b) Squeeze half a lemon into each of the two mason jars. To use as a garnish, slice two circles from the remaining half of the lemon.
To each mason jar, pour 1.5 ounces of Zubrowka. Before pouring in the club soda, add a quarter teaspoon of ginger to each cup. Fill the glass halfway with seltzer water. Enjoy with a lemon slice as a garnish!

93. Vegan Kefir

Makes about 1 quart/liter

Ingredients:
- 1 quart (or liter) filtered water
- ½ cup raw, unsalted cashews
- 1 teaspoon coconut sugar, pure maple syrup, or agave nectar
- 1 tablespoon kefir grains
- Mandarin sections for garnish (optional)

Directions:

a) In a blender, blend together the water, cashews, and coconut sugar (or maple syrup or agave nectar) until it is smooth and creamy.

b) Pour the cashew milk into a 1½- to 2-quart glass jar, making sure that it is less than $2/3$ full. Add the kefir grains, stir, and place the cap on the jar.

c) Leave the jar at room temperature for twenty-four to forty-eight hours, gently agitating it periodically. The cashew milk will become somewhat bubbly, then it will begin to coagulate and separate; simply shake it to remix the kefir, or scoop out the thicker curds and use them as you would use soft cheese or sour cream.

d) Refrigerate for up to one week. When ready to serve the kefir, pour it into a glass and garnish the rim of the glass with mandarin sections, if desired.

94. Black Tea Kombucha

Makes about 3½ quarts/liters

Ingredients:
- 4 quarts (or liters) filtered water
- 1 cup unrefined sugar
- 4 black tea bags or 4 heaping teaspoons loose-leaf tea
- 1 kombucha starter culture

Directions:

a) In a large stainless-steel pot, bring the water to a boil, add the sugar, and stir until the sugar is fully dissolved.

b) Add the black tea bags or loose tea, and boil for an additional 10 minutes to kill off any unwanted microbes that may be present on the tea bags.

c) Turn off the heat, and allow the tea to steep for 15 minutes; remove the tea bags.

d) Allow the tea to cool to room temperature or slightly lukewarm temperature; it should be no warmer than about 70ºF or 21ºC to ensure that the kombucha culture is not damaged.

e) Pour the steeped tea into a large ceramic crock or wide-mouthed glass water jug, such as those used to make iced tea.

f) Add to the tea the kombucha starter culture along with any tea it came with.

g) Cover the top of the crock or jug with a piece of clean linen or cotton (avoid using cheesecloth, as it is too porous), and attach an elastic band around the rim to hold the cloth in place; alternatively, you can use tape around the edge to hold the cloth in place and ensure that the cloth doesn't fall into the crock or jug.

h) Place the crock or jug someplace quiet with air ventilation, in a warm but not sunlit area, where it will not be disturbed.

i) The ideal fermentation temperature range is 73 to 82ºF, or 23 to 28ºC. Once you've located a spot for it, do not move the crock or jug while the kombucha is fermenting, as it may interfere with the culturing process.

j) Wait about five to six days to harvest your kombucha. First, check the taste: If it is sweeter than you'd like, allow it to ferment another day or two. If it has a vinegary taste, you may need to bottle future batches after fermenting a shorter period of time; it is still fine to drink, but you may need to dilute it with water when you drink it to avoid irritating your throat or stomach.
k) Pour all but approximately 2 cups of your fermented kombucha into a glass jar, a container with a lid, or multiple single-serving resealable glass jars (old-fashioned soda pop bottles with the flip-top lid work well), cover, and store it in the refrigerator.

95. African Red Tea Kombucha

Makes about 3½ quarts/liters
Ingredients:
- 4 quarts filtered water
- 1 cup coconut sugar
- 4 teaspoons rooibos loose-leaf tea or 4 rooibos tea bags
- 1 kombucha starter culture

Directions:
a) In a large stainless-steel pot, bring the water to a boil, add the sugar, and stir until the sugar is fully dissolved.
b) Add the rooibos tea bags or loose tea, and boil for an additional 10 minutes to kill off any unwanted microbes that may be present on the tea bags. Turn off the heat, and allow the tea to steep for 15 minutes; remove the tea bags.
c) Let the tea cool to room temperature or slightly lukewarm temperature; it should be no warmer than about 70ºF or 21ºC to ensure that the kombucha culture is not damaged.
d) Pour the steeped tea into a large ceramic crock or wide-mouthed glass water jug, through a fine-mesh sieve in order to remove any loose-leaf tea (if using).
e) Add to the tea the kombucha starter culture along with any tea it came with. Cover the top of the crock or jug with a piece of clean linen or cotton (avoid using cheesecloth, as it is too porous), and attach an elastic band around the rim to hold the cloth in place; alternatively, you can use tape around the edge to hold the cloth in place and ensure that the cloth doesn't fall into the crock or jug.
f) Place the crock or jug someplace quiet with air ventilation, in a warm but not sunlit area, where it will not be disturbed. The ideal fermentation temperature range is 73 to 82ºF, or 23 to 28ºC. Once you've located a spot for it, do not move the crock or jug while the kombucha is fermenting, as it may interfere with the culturing process.

g) Wait about five to six days to harvest your kombucha. First, check the taste: If it is sweeter than you'd like, allow it to ferment another day or two. If it has a vinegary taste, you may need to bottle future batches after a shorter period of time; it is still fine to drink, but you may need to dilute it with water when you drink it to avoid irritating your throat or stomach.

h) Pour all but approximately 2 cups of your fermented kombucha into a glass jar or container with a lid, or multiple single-serving resealable glass jars (old-fashioned soda pop bottles with the flip-top lid work well), cover, and store it in the refrigerator.

i) To increase its fizziness, add a pinch of sugar, and wait another a day or two to drink it. If you keep it longer than a week, you may need to loosen the lid in the fridge to allow gases to escape and prevent the glass from breaking due to excess pressure that may occur over longer periods of time.

96. <u>Cultured Bloody Mary</u>

Makes about 2 cups

Ingredients:
- 4 medium tomatoes
- Juice from ½ lime
- ⅓ cup brine from kimchi, sauerkraut, or pickles
- Dash unrefined sea salt
- Dash pepper
- 1 stalk celery (optional, for garnish)

Directions:
a) In a blender, combine all the ingredients except the celery, and blend until it is smooth.
b) Pour the mixture into a covered glass dish, and allow it to ferment for two to twelve hours, depending on your preference; longer fermentation times result in a tangier drink.
c) Garnish with celery if desired, and serve immediately.
d) Store any leftovers in a jar in the fridge for up to three days.

97. Peach Iced Tea

INGREDIENTS:
- 4 black tea bags
- 8 cups water
- 1/2 cup peach syrup
- 1/2 cup honey
- Sliced peaches (optional)
- Mint leaves (optional)

INSTRUCTIONS:
a) Brew the tea bags in 8 cups of boiling water for 5 minutes.
b) Remove the tea bags and stir in the peach syrup and honey until dissolved.
c) Let the tea cool to room temperature.
d) Fill Mason jars with ice, and pour the tea over the ice.
e) Add sliced peaches and mint leaves for garnish, if desired.
f) Serve and enjoy!

98. Watermelon Agua Fresca

INGREDIENTS:
- 4 cups chopped watermelon
- 2 cups water
- 1/4 cup lime juice
- 1/4 cup honey
- Mint leaves (optional)

INSTRUCTIONS:
a) Add the watermelon, water, lime juice, and honey to a blender.
b) Blend until smooth.
c) Fill Mason jars with ice, and pour the agua fresca over the ice.
d) Add mint leaves for garnish, if desired.
e) Serve and enjoy!

99. <u>Blueberry Lemonade</u>

INGREDIENTS:
- 1 cup blueberries
- 1/2 cup lemon juice
- 1/2 cup honey
- 6 cups water
- Lemon slices (optional)
- Blueberries (optional)

INSTRUCTIONS:
a) Add the blueberries, lemon juice, and honey to a blender.
b) Blend until smooth.
c) Strain the mixture through a fine mesh strainer.
d) Fill Mason jars with ice, and pour the blueberry lemonade over the ice.
e) Add lemon slices and blueberries for garnish, if desired.
f) Serve and enjoy!

100. **Mango Lassi**

INGREDIENTS:
- 1 cup plain yogurt
- 1 cup chopped fresh mango
- 1/4 cup honey
- 1/4 cup milk
- 1/4 tsp ground cardamom
- Mint leaves (optional)

INSTRUCTIONS:
a) Add the yogurt, mango, honey, milk, and cardamom to a blender.
b) Blend until smooth.
c) Fill Mason jars with ice, and pour the mango lassi over the ice.
d) Add mint leaves for garnish, if desired.
e) Serve and enjoy!

CONCLUSION

In conclusion, mason jar meals are a versatile and convenient way to enjoy healthy and delicious food anytime, anywhere. By using mason jars for food storage and serving, you can easily portion out meals and snacks, and take them with you on the go. With endless possibilities for recipes, mason jar meals are a perfect solution for busy individuals who want to eat healthy without sacrificing taste or convenience. So next time you're looking for a quick and easy meal prep option, try making a mason jar meal and enjoy the benefits of this innovative trend.

www.ingramcontent.com/pod-product-compliance
Lightning Source LLC
Chambersburg PA
CBHW070413120526
44590CB00014B/1383